Italian
HIDEAWAYS

Italian HIDEAWAYS

DISCOVERING ENCHANTING ROOMS *and* PRIVATE VILLAS

MEG NOLAN

PHOTOGRAPHY BY

DAVID CICCONI

RIZZOLI
NEW YORK

First published in the United States of America in 2008
by Rizzoli International Publications, Inc.
300 Park Avenue South
New York, NY 10010
www.rizzoliusa.com

2008 2009 2010 2011 / 10 9 8 7 6 5 4 3 2 1

Distributed in the U.S. trade by Random House, New York

Printed in China

ISBN-10: 0-8478-3104-3
ISBN-13: 978-0-8478-3104-3

Library of Congress Control Number: 2007940041

 ROBERTO COIN

CONTENTS

Foreword   vi

Introduction   1

LAZIO
    La Posta Vecchia   6
    Il Palazzetto   14
    Portrait Suites   18

TOSCANA
    Villa Fontelunga   24
    Castello del Nero   30
    Castello Banfi: Il Borgo   36
    Albergo Villa Marta   40
    Villa Cabbiavoli   48
    La Bandita   54
    Il Falconiere   62
    Villa Castelletto   68
    Castello di Vicarello   74
    Villa Mangiacane   82
    Hotel Lungarno   88
    Torre di Bellosguardo   94

PUGLIA
    Masseria Torre Coccaro   102
    Masseria Torre Maizza   108
    La Sommita   112

PIEMONTE
    Villa Beccaris   118
    Villa Tiboldi   124
    La Villa Hotel   130

CAMPANIA
    JK Capri   136
    Villa Cimbrone   144
    Casa Angelina   150
    Mezzatorre   156

VENETO
    Ca Maria Adele   162
    Palazzo Bauer   168
    Palazzo Mocenigo   176

LE MARCHE
    Carducci 76   182

UMBRIA
    Borgo di Bastia Creti   188

Hotel Appendix   195
Acknowledgments   197
About the Author   199

FOREWORD

MELISSA BIGGS BRADLEY

IN one of my all-time favorite novels, *A Soldier of the Great War*, by Mark Helprin, the novel's protagonist is described as a man who "liked to know where he was in the world and what was around him. A map...was for him what a Bible was for a priest, a book for an intellectual, and so forth." A few pages later, this protagonist sets forth his theory of Italy, the setting of his tale. "Though Italy is flanked on three sides by the sea, and in the north by a mountain barrier, and though its early history is an illustration of the success of uniform administration and centralism, this country has exemplified division, contention, and atomization. Mind you, for art, for the development of the soul, nothing is better than a landscape of separate and impregnable towers. The variety, the sense of possibility, and the watchfulness that such an environment creates have given to us many honors unparalleled in the world."

More succinctly, Umberto Eco has declared that Italy is a "country dominated by difference and by a taste for proportion." In fact, Eco has claimed that Italy's landscape is so varied that every five kilometers one encounters a new country. I believe that such contrasts and diversity are the secret behind its magnetic pull on the tourist. No matter how many times one visits Italy, the desire to return remains—is even enhanced—because each journey offers so many new possibilities. The first time I visited Florence and glimpsed some of its Renaissance masterpieces, I left determined to see Rome. After touring Venice, I longed to return to tour Verona and the Palladian villas. A few weeks in Sicily and I grew intrigued by tales of Naples and Puglia. Each visit provokes a new wish list.

Staying in small, tucked-away hotels or renting a private villa is clearly one of the most authentic and inspiring ways to obtain an intimate view of Italy and her many-faceted charms. Whether it be escaping to an all-white, modern cliffside dwelling on the famed Amalfi Coast, like Casa Angelina, or to a restored country villa nestled among the rich vineyards of Piemonte, such as Villa Tiboldi, or to the designer-inspired hotel Carducci 76, which is hidden in a small beach town on the Adriatic, there's a stunning range of unforgettable vistas and indigenous style in Italy available to the modern traveler.

In *Italian Hideaways*, Meg Nolan has selected thirty properties spanning the country-from Puglia to the Veneto-that showcase the best of Italy's smaller hotels and private villas. Among them there is a remarkably consistent high level of design, but also a great variety of taste. All are artfully presented and noted for their privacy and discreet locations-just the kind of properties where one can truly hide away. However, she has also included two larger urban hotels with memorable rooms, which sufficiently captivate and envelop the guest to qualify as hideaways as well.

As Helprin's soldier claimed, Italy remains a country of honors and pleasures unparalleled, so it will forever entice and stimulate visitors. With twenty separate regions, each with its own alluring traits and quirks, the country is a touchstone for insatiable travelers like myself. It is also an unending source of inspiration for me as a traveler, a journalist, and a pleasure seeker. I have spent much of my professional life unearthing special hotels and insider travel tips so that I may share my discoveries and help others make remarkable journeys. It is clear from the treasures revealed in these pages that Meg Nolan shares this mission and this passion for travel and for Italy.

The homegrown delights of Castello di Vicarello

INTRODUCTION

I first traveled to Italy in 1997. My parents had planned a spectacular tour of some of the country's best spots. The three-week adventure was my first introduction to *la bella vita*, and its brilliant impression was without a doubt what spurred my successive years of studying, working, and now writing about Italy. For me, the highlight of the trip was actually our first stop—the Grand Hotel Villa Serbelloni, which is located in the small town of Bellagio, known as the pearl of Italy's famed Lake Como. After a harrowing drive along the narrow, cliff-hugging road that stretches along the east side of the lake, we arrived at perhaps the most magnificent building I had ever seen. Majestic with its antique yellow facade and lakefront location, the Villa Serbelloni awed me with its profound beauty and prominence. Then we went inside. The decadence of the villa's interiors was simply overwhelming. Although I was fortunate enough to have visited stunning homes and hotels in the United States, nothing had quite prepared me for the old-world, nineteenth-century Italian standard of opulence on display here. High, frescoed ceilings, a glorious marble staircase with gilded floor chandeliers, and two enormous salons filled with neoclassical antiques and Persian rugs left me speechless. The Imperial stone terrace overlooking the lake and the gardens held such romance that my eighteen-year-old imagination was sent into overdrive.

The garden terrace and boat dock at the Grand Hotel Serbelloni

Our room, though, was the most memorable element of the entire vacation. Upgraded to one of the villa's two Grand Suites, my family and I found ourselves unpacking our bags and battling our jetlag in the lavish lap of luxury. The suite featured a large bedroom with a lounge area, a small dressing room, two bathrooms, and a sitting room with a large window overlooking the lake, where my brother, sister, and I slept, spoiled beyond our years. The room's dimensions were of palatial proportions, with tall ceilings and floor-to-ceiling balcony windows. Fine antiques and silk curtains complemented the regal décor, which also included a full wall of arched antique mirrors and massive marble columns. The room was one I will never forget, not only because of its opulent furnishings and historic splendor but also because of the way it made all of us feel. Inside this glorious massive villa we had found ourselves a private enclave in which we were able to unwind and feel comfortable despite our extravagant surroundings. For me, this feeling of sanctuary was what resonated most from the experience and is what I have looked to re-create with every future hotel stay in my life.

Traveling through Italy to research and photograph a select number of its small hotels and private villas for this book has been perhaps the most illuminating and constructive phase in my longstanding affair with Italy. The central purpose of the book is to illustrate the wide variety of

Italy's smaller and lesser-known hotels and private villas, and particularly those outside the tourist-heavy regions. There were more than enough wonderful spots to choose from; it was narrowing them down while ensuring that Italy's impressive and diverse landscapes and design styles were well documented that provided the challenge. For weeks on end I scoured the country for its best-kept, most enchanting secrets, feeling simultaneously elated and motivated by each new discovery. Unfortunately I couldn't include every hideaway I found, and often otherwise extraordinary hotels and villas, though beautiful, simply didn't fit the book's mandate. The larger hotels I have included—like Hotel Lungarno and the Palazzo Bauer—may have worldwide reputations but, like the Grand Hotel Serbelloni, have certain rooms that still maintain a sanctuary quality through their unique views, décor, and setting within the hotel.

During the research tours for the book, I returned to visit the Grand Hotel Villa Serbelloni. The main floor remains much the same with the staircase and front salons, but extensive changes have been made to the ground floor with the addition of a restaurant, indoor pool, and full-service spa. And alas, the original stone terrace has also been altered and now is encased in glass, with a retractable roof. Fortunately, though, no refurbishment or modern addition can affect the villa's remarkable view. The sheer, gray Alpine peaks still loom over the lake, creating a dramatic visual as they rise up from the deep blue waters. The lush green mountainside and colorful stone buildings along the opposite lakeshore paint a striking contrast against the calm lapis water. This truly magical view has had a magnetic and profound effect on me over the years. Not only has it tempted me to return, but it is also what has compelled me to journey farther into Italy, fueled by a passion to discover more and more of the enchanting places I know to exist in the country I fell in love with years ago.

ABOVE *The Grand Hotel Serbelloni's lakefront prominence*

OPPOSITE *French doors open onto the lake in a Deluxe Room*

ABOVE *The palatial sitting room outside the executive suite* | OPPOSITE *The preferred way to travel across the lake*

LA POSTA VECCHIA

QUITE possibly one of the most refined and exclusive hideaways in Italy owing to its venerable past owners, La Posta Vecchia exudes a sort of singular authenticity unlike other historic hotels. Its seaside position, towering above the crashing surf of the Tyrrhenian Sea, just twenty-five miles northwest of Rome, lends a breathtaking romance to the ancient Roman building. Long, rectangular, and bookended by two steeples, the peach-colored villa is a sight to behold. Set upon lush, landscaped Mediterranean-style gardens and with a spectacular firework-shaped palm tree at its noble entrance, the villa makes an arresting first impression. The stone driveway cuts through eucalyptus bushes and hedgerow-protected herb gardens, ending ceremoniously at two massive wooden doors that mark the entrance. A smock-clad staff member stands just outside the doors, poised to greet and unload the luggage. Marvelously sheltered, the villa is cushioned on either side by a World Wildlife Foundation Bird Sanctuary and Palo Castle, a magnificent second century castle complete with storybook turrets that is still owned by the same family who built the villa.

The Posta Vecchia was constructed in 1640 by the Odescalchi family as a hostel for the many visitors and tradesmen traveling to visit them at Palo Castle. In 1918, the Post House Inn (*La Posta Vecchia*) closed its doors and was left neglected until the early 1960s, when American Jean Paul Getty rented the villa from his good friend Prince Ladislao Odescalchi and then ultimately convinced him to part with it. Getty restored the villa and its gardens, converting it into his own luxurious seaside manor. During the villa's refurbishment, workers uncovered ruins from two ancient Roman villas dating back to the second century B.C. With such extraordinary historical relics as original Etruscan artifacts and mosaic floors buried beneath the villa, the Italian government swooped in and together with Getty created the Archeological Museum, now housed below the villa. In 1976, when Getty passed away, La Posta Vecchia was bought by a Swiss hotel company and offered as a private villa rental. Then in 1990 it was converted into a luxury hotel. The hotel continues to restore the collection of Roman art discovered on site with the help of the Gruppo Archeologico del Territorio Cerite, which offers guided tours of the museum and the ruins scattered throughout the property on Tuesday afternoons. The museum, however, is open every day and easily accessible to guests from a staircase near the entrance hall.

La Posta Vecchia's most enviable feature, though there are many, may very well be the long stone terrace above the water's edge. At one end, just outside the indoor pool, are several lounge chairs for sunbathing, and at the other end is a classic black-and-white-striped bench cushion, emblematic of the hotel's genuine chic. White

Bathed in moonlight, La Posta Vecchia's ancient ruins

canvas umbrellas shade tables and chairs where, weather permitting, both lunch and dinner are served. Such expansive views and intimate seating by the sea give the villa its timeless appeal. The ground floor of the villa, including the entrance hall, is one continuous space, with each room unfolding into the next. Buffered on each end by the elegant formal restaurant and an indoor pool, the interior rooms are made up of salons, libraries, and a peach-colored breakfast room. The décor is filled with magnificent tapestries, ancient stone and marble tables, and various precious Roman artifacts. Elegant touches like a piano player during cocktail hour, and the hotel's informal "honesty bar" in the library, where miniature glass bottles of mixers and high-end spirits are tucked into the bookshelves, keep the villa feeling intimate and personal. Imagining a better place to court someone is a challenge.

Daily activities such as cooking classes, complimentary round-trip transportation to Rome, and bicycles are readily available to guests. Oasi di Palo, a wooded park owned by the World Wildlife Fund, is right next to the property and has hiking paths, jogging trails, and an athletic center that includes tennis courts and soccer fields. There is also a small beauty center that offers massages and beauty treatments overlooking the sea. Dining at La Posta Vecchia's formal Ceasar restaurant—a vaulted dining room with Fortuny fabric drapes alongside massive full-length windows with views out to the sea—is an exquisite affair. The menu is directed by a talented young chef and enhanced by the hotel's extensive vegetable and herb gardens. Decadent options like lobster and white truffles feature prominently, and dessert is worth saving room for, with homemade gelato and delicious flourless chocolate cake. The hotel's emphasis on leisure is overwhelming, so it is best to simply embrace it and relax in its extraordinary lap of luxury.

THE ROOMS

Each of La Posta Vecchia's nineteen rooms is decorated individually and named after either famous past guests or its stunning view. Furnished with Roman artifacts and artwork found by J. P. Getty with the help of Professor Federico Zeri, curator at the time of the Getty Museum in Los Angeles, each of the oversize rooms conveys an authentic grandeur not easily found in today's hotels. The heavy antique furniture draped in seventeenth-century fabric seems almost demure beneath the tall ceilings and floor-length window terraces looking out over the sea. The gilded beds are stately, opulent affairs with large ornamental bed frames and tapestry canopies. The linens are high quality, and the bathrooms are rich in marble or tile with original bronze fixtures and marble vanities. Each room comes with plush terry bathrobes, Bulgari-brand bath products, and satellite-equipped televisions with DVD players. The decadence of the rooms is made ever more compelling by the constant sound of the Tyrrhenian Sea just below.

The Castello Suite has perhaps the best view, with two large windows opening over the sea to the horizon and another two facing the resplendent yet still formidable-looking Odescalchi castle next door. The unorthodox pairing of a bright yellow couch and a jade green carpet appears noble within the grand dimensions of the room. The authentic elements of an ornate stone fireplace and a gilded Venetian floor lamp keep the room true to its historic roots. Each room is a marvel waiting to be explored, with distinct treasures and details separating them from one another. The larger suites offer a truly luxurious experience, but the deluxe rooms are equally impressive. The Duke's Room, the only double with a view of the sea, features a particularly attractive tapestry over the bed and brightly tiled bathroom. The rooms over the sea, though, are the main attraction, with the constant crashing of the waves providing the ideal lullaby for a blissful night's sleep.

The rarefied interiors of the ancient Post House Inn

OVERLEAF
The impressive façade (left); The Castello Suite

ABOVE *Seaside serenity on the terrace* | OPPOSITE *Al fresco dining with the imposing Odescalchi Castle in the background*

IL PALAZZETTO

ROMA, LAZIO

VIRTUALLY hidden inside Rome's famed Spanish Steps, this small hotel has just four bedrooms, guaranteeing its exclusivity among the grand hotels of the Eternal City. The square, villalike building tucked behind the wall of the steps was built in 1500. It was the preferred retreat of a noble Roman family who favored the ensconced location of Il Palazzetto to their grand palace in Piazza Mignanelli. Today, the historic structure belongs to Hotel Hassler owner Roberto E. Wirth, who bought the property with the intention of offering his hotel guests something elite. The ground floor of the hotel is the home base of the International Wine Academy of Roma, a wine club founded and presided over by Wirth where members and guests meet to enjoy the grape's finest triumphs. Due to its exclusive nature and small number of rooms, booking for rooms and dinner at Il Palazzetto and the International Wine Academy of Roma requires considerable planning, though it is well worth it.

Il Palazzetto also has its own restaurant and adjacent wine bar that provide a welcome respite from the crowds out on the steps and soothe the patron with a rich red palette and fine Roman cuisine. With a wine list offering more than four hundred labels and resident experts on staff, a glass of great wine is unavoidable. The restaurant offers two dining areas. The first is in the charming and intimate library, with wall-to-

Spiral staircase in Rome's hidden gem: Il Palazzetto

wall books and a large fireplace. The second is the hotel's very own secret garden. The entrance is just through the back doors on the ground floor and is most often used for private dinners and events. The garden's ivy-covered walls, potted plants, and lulling stone fountain create a relaxing, pleasant environment.

The terraces of Il Palazzetto are the hotel's true draw. Located on the fourth and fifth floors, dangling over the Spanish Steps, they are fabulous places to savor remarkable fine wines and local fare. Often used for private events, the red-+ awning-covered dining terrace can accommodate up to fifty people. The spectacular view from the terraces includes all there is to be seen in the immediate vicinity: the Spanish Steps, Piazza di Spagna (including a bird's-eye view of the Barcaccia fountain), the Trinita dei Monti Church, and the obelisk at the head of the steps. The experience is simply unforgettable.

Two entrances to the hotel are not only convenient for the guest but also provide dual opportunity for drumming up intrigue and perhaps a bit of envy from onlookers. The double-iron-gated entrance onto the fifth-floor terrace is perhaps the more exclusive of the two entrances. Located just to the right of the Piazza Santa Trinita dei Monti at the top of the Spanish Steps, the tall ivy-covered archway and miniscule plaque on the side of the door tantalize all who walk by. A buzzer intercom system permits fortunate guests to enter into the

THE ROOMS

private haven, leaving the crowds and the gaping passersby in their wake.

Owing to Il Palazzetto's petite size, guests are invited to use the facilities of the nearby (just two minutes away) Hotel Hassler. Undeniably one of the grandest hotels in Rome, the Hassler's five-star services include a wellness center, panoramic terrace on the seventh floor, business center, and full buffet breakfast, all open to Palazzetto guests. Whether the draw of this little hideaway is the wine, the terrace, or simply the rare experience of staying in one of Rome's true hidden gems, the time spent at Il Palazzetto is a luxurious affair.

The four boutique suites at Il Palazzetto were all decorated personally by Roberto's wife, Astrid, who used a hybrid of neoclassical and contemporary styles. Located on the third and fourth floors, each room overlooks the Spanish Steps, creating an immediate intimacy with the city at large. Done in supple beiges and creams with luxurious fabrics like velvet and satin and well-appointed furnishings, the rooms are remarkably comfortable, with down comforters and big full mattresses. Each room comes equipped with modern amenities—a flat-screen television with satellite service, Internet hook-up, a mini-bar, and air-conditioning, leaving the guest to want for nothing. Room 4 (pictured above) features two large shuttered windows that open directly out to the steps and a big marble bathroom well suited to dressing for an evening out on the town.

ABOVE *The pleasing palette of Il Palazzetto's rooms*

OPPOSITE *The intimate view from the terrace*

PORTRAIT SUITES

*L*IKE stepping into a stylish friend's flat in the most posh neighborhood of the city, Portrait Suites would leave you green with envy if it weren't for the fact that you're invited to treat your room like it's your own. It's no wonder many of Potrait Suites' guests have turned into month-long residents, hesitant to relinquish their swish pad in Rome's high-end shopping area. Just minutes from the Piazza di Spagna, the boutique hotel's convenient location is just a precursor for the overall tranquil experience presented by the hotel. The calm sensibility of Portrait Suites begins at check-in, when instead of being confronted with a desk and a harried receptionist the guest is ushered into a comfortable and well-appointed sitting room. Framed prints of fashion models along with a complimentary beverage tray offering a cool glass of water or juice serve to casually distract the guest from any possible wait time. The few staff members introduce themselves by name and appear sincere when they guide you to your room and tell you they are there to help you with whatever you may need.

The hotel is the latest addition to the Lungarno Hotels group, owned and managed by the Ferragamo family. Unlike the Ferragamos' other properties, mostly all in Florence, Portrait Suites leaves no guesswork as to who is behind the luxe design. Photographs and sketches done by Salvatore Ferragamo line the walls of the

The Ferragamo legacy on display on the walls of the Suite

staircase, making the walk up and down from the room or the terrace infinitely more interesting than the elevator. Due to the hotel's fashion-minded owners and designers, the décor of the hotel is anything but an afterthought.

In a city where the rooftops are often more lavishly adorned than the buildings' interiors, and certainly more intriguing, the icing on Portrait Suite's artfully designed cake is its chic rooftop terrace. The rooftop is open to all guests at all hours and has an "honesty bar" where no type or brand of beverage seems to be missing. Deep-cushioned chair and sofa sets complete with large umbrellas make it the ideal lounge area for eating breakfast, reading, spying on the neighbors, or simply appreciating the fantastic view of the magnificent ancient city. For dining, the hotel offers only a complimentary breakfast, but its convenient location to a local market, some of the city's top restaurants, and multiple *enotecas* makes finding special lunch and dinner options easy.

THE ROOMS

The fourteen suites range in category from classic rooms to a two-bedroom suite, though all come with the signature style you would expect from a hotel associated with the Ferragamo brand. Memorable details include cotton fringe curtains lined in lime silk panels and bright-pink

throw pillows on the contemporary-style sofas and chairs. Of course, this being a Ferragamo operation, leather features heavily in the design style and furnishings. Leather-covered stools and long benches at the foot of the beds keep the overall aesthetic fresh and clean. Even the desktops have high-quality leather blotters. The guest rooms' best feature (and the reason guests often opt to extend their stay) is the full-service kitchenette. Large dark wooden doors slide back to reveal a stainless-steel kitchenette built into the wall, complete with cupboards and a counter and sink. It comes outfitted with both a modern push-button espresso maker as well as a traditional French press. There is a well-stocked fridge plus all sorts of light snacks, as well as cutlery, plates, and glasses sufficient for two. The real luxury, however, is the built-in dishwasher. The kitchenette renders the guest so self-sufficient that the hotel's lack of a restaurant is hardly a problem. Room 53 is a "deluxe" room and one of the two rooms with a private balcony, the other being the magnificent penthouse suite, whose terrace wraps around the entire front of the building and offers a truly indulgent and private view of the Piazza di Spagna and frenetic well-heeled Rome below.

ABOVE *Top views from Portrait Suites roof deck*

OPPOSITE *Modern sophistication in the sitting room*

CLOCKWISE FROM TOP LEFT
*The central covered staircase;
cork detail in a guestroom;
original print curtains in a
guestroom*

OPPOSITE *The unassuming
entrance of Portrait Suites*

VILLA FONTELUNGA *and*

VILLA SCANNAGALLO, VILLA GALLO, *and* VILLA GALLETTO

POZZO DELLA CHIANA (FOIANO), TOSCANA

CONCEIVED and decorated by a former movie set designer, Villa Fontelunga and, even more so, its separate concierge villas, Villa Scannagallo, Villa Gallo, and Villa Galletto, appear ready for their close-ups. A former Padronale villa, Fontelunga enjoys a prominent hilltop position with views down the valley, situated as it is in Tuscany's Val di Chiana area, best known for its designer outlet shops, just under an hour from Florence and only thirty minutes to the gorgeous Etruscan hill town of Cortona. Carefully blending the traditional look of the box-shaped villa with contemporary design details and furnishings, the three owners, Simon, Philip, and Paolo, work tirelessly to make their home seem like it's yours. The villa's warm presentation and genteel character are a direct reflection of the charming men who built and run it.

Driving up to the main villa may seem daunting from a map's perspective, but the reality is a pleasant country drive guided by white painted signs with the villa's name written in its signature swirling cursive script leading the way from the nearest village. Villa Fontelunga is a gorgeous blush pink color with light-blue shutters, meticulous landscaping, and terra-cotta-potted geraniums on the back veranda. The terra-cotta-tiled pool is down the hill a bit from the villa, providing a restful lounging experience with no distraction from your book other than the sound of birds chirping or the exceptional

Backyard bathing at Villa Fontelunga

garden view. The main villa (Villa Fontelunga) sleeps eighteen people at maximum and can be rented out exclusively for private events. The majority of the time, Villa Fontelunga is run as a delightful B&B with a homemade buffet breakfast and family-style dinners served twice a week. The kitchen, dining, and sitting area are all melded together in one big open space with three sets of French doors leading out to a few tables and chairs shaded by large white umbrellas. The view from the outdoor tables makes ordering a second cappuccino at breakfast and maybe just one more homemade pastry feel guilt-free. There is no formal restaurant, so lunch and most evenings' dinners are left up to the guests. Fortunately, the local town offers a few fabulous options, and an evening in nearby Cortona can be a special treat.

THE ROOMS

The nine guest rooms of Villa Fontelunga are done in jewel themes with a mix of antique and contemporary furnishings. Each room is named after a semiprecious stone and decorated in the corresponding color scheme. The amethyst room is a particular favorite; its sheer violet curtains give an ethereal glow to the morning sunlight. Each room comes with its own CD player, telephone, and free wireless service. There is a junior suite tangential to the main building with French

doors out to its own terrace overlooking the pool and an enormous oak tree.

The concierge villas are set in the neighboring valley, a ten-minute walk or two-minute drive from Fontelunga. Available for weekly rental, the villas are brand-new structures conceived and built by the three owners. The largest, Scannagallo, sleeps up to ten; the two smaller villas, Gallo and Galletto, sleep four and two respectively. The villas are laid out so that the two smaller share a pool and face each other diagonally, while Scannagallo is twenty yards away with its own spectacular infinity pool. The interiors of the two villas have a playful yet sophisticated flourish to them. Each bedroom is done in a monochromatic color scheme so that bedspreads match the headboards, which also match the chairs and the curtains. The walls are all painted a simple cream color, relying on a mix of colorful poster prints to tie in to the room's color schemes. The architecture of the smaller villas is very contemporary, with full walls of sliding glass doors creating convertible indoor-to-outdoor living rooms, exposed ceiling beams, and exposed brick walls. The furnishings all work with the notion of less is more, leaving the stylish flair of the owners

to present itself through humorous design elements like two large antique clock hands nailed to the living room wall that point to 5 o'clock on the painted clock face and with the question "Cocktails?" written in the same swirling cursive of the Fontelunga signs below. In fact, the flowery penmanship belongs to Philip, one of the three owners, and the main interior designer of the group. He found the massive clock hands and knew they had to go somewhere. He now muses that the question mark after cocktails should perhaps be an exclamation point instead. The three villas come with cleaning staff, groceries, and access to the vast DVD and CD libraries of Villa Fontelunga. The plantings around the villas, particularly the ever-abundant lavender plants, keep the bees buzzing and the grounds wonderfully fragrant. The yellow and green fields just beyond the manicured properties provide ample pensive moments, while the outdoor dining gazebo seems ripe for a raucous meal shared with friends. The most remarkable element of the villas is that despite their contemporary design they sink effortlessly into the traditional and classical landscape as if they had always been there.

ABOVE *The valley view from Villa Fontelunga (left); the architect's visionary modern pool at Villa Scannagallo (right)*

OPPOSITE *The whimsical flair of Villa Fontelunga's interior design*

OVERLEAF *Interiors and the view from the concierge villas: Villa Galletto, Scannagallo, and Gallo*

CASTELLO DEL NERO

TAVARNELLE VAL DI PESA, TOSCANA

LOCATED an hour from Florence and Siena, Castello del Nero offers the seclusion of a private villa with the high-end services of a luxury hotel. With one of only two E'SPA-brand spas in Tuscany, Castello del Nero distinguishes itself as a property dedicated to pampered relaxation. In addition to the spa's services, the castle offers fine dining on the terrace overlooking the iconic rolling hills and leisurely strolls through the manicured rose gardens and magnificent frescoed chapel. Both the restored chapel with vaulted ceilings and the garden's ancient trees, featuring a cedar over 400 years old and clusters of 150-year-old cypress, root the refurbished twelfth-century castle in its historic past.

The castle was originally owned by the noble Del Nero family, former mayors of Florence, and then in 1825 it was sold to the noble Torrigiani family. Today, Castello del Nero is under the protection and watchful eye of the Italian Fine Arts Commission, which has helped amass and uncover an impressive art collection among the castle's original holdings. The objects and paintings scattered throughout the property's common rooms and suites are of considerable historic value. The dedication to the preservation and appreciation of the castle's noble past is apparent at check-in. The immense lobby area, with its vaulted ceilings, arched doorways, and terra-cotta floors, has a grand, opulent flair. The

The noble crest in the Gallway Suite at Castello del Nero

service at Castello del Nero is reminiscent of a five-star city hotel where your wish is their command and everything is done promptly and as precisely as possible—a rare delight in rural Italy.

The layout of the hotel is surprising. What appears rectangular and straightforward is in fact full of angles and dead ends, making arriving at the bar before dinner an adventure. Fortunately, the bar is housed in the old kitchen, and its long wooden bar, exposed stone walls, and large fireplace make it a most welcoming destination. The meals at Castello del Nero are hearty and meant to reflect the surrounding area's bounty. Homemade pastries and breads tempt at each sitting, while organically grown vegetables help keep those on a diet in line. On some nights there is a theme to the dinner, like an all-meat roast that includes not only the expected beef and chicken but also local pheasant, venison, and wild boar. The wine list is another boastful card in Castello del Nero's stacked hand, featuring more than two hundred local wines and guaranteed to impress even the most astute of wine connoisseurs.

Day trips to Florence and Siena from the castle are made simple with complimentary shuttles. It's pulling oneself away from the spa and pool that requires effort. The spa, located on the lower level of the hotel and with separate entrance out to the pool, is perhaps the best reason to spend a long weekend at Castello del Nero. The hotel's spa is considered to be the top spa in

THE ROOMS

It's difficult to decide what the most appealing feature of the fifty varying rooms and suites at Castello del Nero is—the expansive views of the cypress trees, olive groves, and vineyards, or the unbelievably comfortable beds. The view is perhaps more memorable, given its distinctive quality, but the beds at Castello del Nero, with their light goose-down duvets, silky-soft linens, cashmere blankets, and brand-new double mattresses (another rarity in Italy), make waking up to the view all the more enjoyable. Each room differs in layout, style, and décor, though the majority feature slanted wood-beamed ceilings, *cotto* (Florentine tile) floors, and bathrooms decorated with mosaics and marble. The décor of the rooms, particularly the color schemes, were chosen to replicate each room's original decoration. In the Gallway Suite, a family crest was repainted above the bed, and the walls and ceiling are covered in frescoes. The grandeur of the suite reflects the noble lineage of its former residents. Hidden doors painted into the wall reveal an atticlike bathroom that despite the slanted ceiling feels spacious and remarkably private. Large shuttered windows with stone benches give the room its authentic appeal, and the massive stone fireplace provides an austere view from the bed. Although designed to echo its rich tradition, the suite has been refurbished to offer luxury amenities like flat-screen television, air-conditioning, Internet access, and movies on demand. The executive suite or Tuscan Room is considerably less opulent and historic than the Gallway. However, its blue-and-white upholstered headboard and Roman-arched doorway give it an appealing, fresh feel while simultaneously maintaining the simplicity of the castle's countryside setting.

the region with specialized treatments including facials, massages, hot stone therapy, and even an Olive Oil and Pink Clay Oriental Inspired Head Massage—making an appointment during your stay a necessary indulgence. Like many hotels in Tuscany, the castle's authenticity seems best appreciated during the hotel's low season. Owner Bob Trotta and his lovely wife, Ragni, cite the beautiful colors of the autumn harvest as the reason fall is one of their favorite times to visit Castello del Nero.

The rich interior of the Gallway Suite

OPPOSITE *The artful design of the garden at Castello del Nero*

CLOCKWISE FROM TOP LEFT
*The cozy grotto-style bar; a
Roman arch in an executive
room; the elegant floral fabric
of the executive room*

OPPOSITE *The unforgettable
view from the dining terrace
overlooking the garden*

CASTELLO BANFI: IL BORGO

MONTALCINO, TOSCANA

Best known for its excellent wines, particularly the Brunello di Montalcino, Castello Banfi is an obligatory stopover for the true oenophile. Originally a medieval fortress, renamed Castello Banfi by its American owners and since refurbished as a hospitality center, the estate is enormous, with 7,100 acres of vineyards, olive groves, fruit orchards, and gardens. The estate offers dining, a historical museum, cooking classes, wine tastings, vineyard treks, and, since March 2007, a private *borgo* with fourteen luxury accommodations complete with an outdoor swimming pool. Castello Banfi also hosts music festivals, both privately and in partnership with nearby Montalcino's summer and winter jazz and wine festivals, ensuring guests will be well-entertained. The prestigious hilltop position of the castle allows for sweeping views of the estate's vineyards and various groves. From the road and the long winding driveway, the castle appears majestic, casting an imperious shadow across the landscape and causing a romantic stirring inside all those arriving at its door. The view from the main castle's western terrace and the *borgo*'s private pool is spectacular at sunset, when hazy hues of pink decorate the sky creating a beautiful contrast against the rolling green vineyards.

The castle's two restaurants, La Taverna and Il Ristorante, provide both informal and formal, Michelin-rated culinary experiences. La Taverna is open to the public for lunch but exclusively to *borgo* guests at dinner, so that guests may have a less formal option than Il Ristorante, which is only open for dinner. The vaulted ceilings beneath the castle's eastern side give La Taverna its rustic ambience, while the robust tasting menu, complete with generous wine pairings and attentive service, promises a sophisticated experience. A dinner at Il Ristorante is an entirely decadent and romantic affair—ideal for a celebration. The five-course meal, served with sumptuous wine pairings, is presented in a dramatic candelit setting on the second floor of the castle. The food is delicious, the wine superb, and the ambience intoxicating, and you can even take the memory home with you in the form of bottles of the castle's award-winning wine.

Just an hour away from Siena and two and a half hours from Florence, the *borgo* at Castello Banfi makes an easy departure point for touring either city by day. Plus, you can take comfort in knowing that when you return home to the *borgo* you are guaranteed a delicious dinner with some of the area's best wine.

THE ROOMS

The *borgo* was refurbished from a cluster of original historic homes built close to the fortress for protection in the seventeenth and eighteenth centuries. The entrance to the *borgo* is just to the left of the fortress's main entrance and is roped off to

The imposing fortress tower at Castello Banfi

CLOCKWISE FROM TOP LEFT
Room 18, a Tuscan-inspired loft; the floral warmth of the guestrooms; the rustic charm of Il Borgo

The acclaimed vineyards of Castello Banfi

ensure privacy from the many daytime visitors to the Banfi Estate. The *borgo* guests have access to all the amenities of the estate but enjoy the privacy of a garden pergola, small gym, and pool, and a full breakfast daily.

Italian interior designer Federico Forquet individually conceptualized the décor of the fourteen rooms at the *borgo*. Each room features a king-sized bed, heavenly after a full day of eating and drinking, and the five suites also have a pull-out queen-sized sofa for any spillover guests or small children. Modern room amenities include flat-screen televisions, stereos, high-speed Internet hook-ups, and mini-bars stocked with the estate's award-winning wines and snacks, including perhaps the most deliciously addictive treat ever: local milk chocolate-covered dried grapes—gourmet Raisinets®.

The rooms are painted in soft pastel colors with fabrics in thick, country-style plaids. The aqua-and-red pattern of room 18 (pictured left) is the most pleasant, and the large white walk-in closet is so well designed you will want to mentally record it for future adaptation back home. Many of the walls are exposed brick, and some, like room 13, have beautiful arched ceilings fortified with the same brick outline. Walk-in closets and spacious bathrooms with tile-and-glass showers make the rooms feel grand without appearing formal or overdone. Large windows with wistful views overlook Banfi's vast vineyards or the scenic downhill driveway lined with cypress trees. The aesthetic is of a luxuriously modernized Tuscan farmhouse just freshly cleaned.

ALBERGO VILLA MARTA

LUCCA, TOSCANA

THIS unassuming cream-colored villa sits amid olive groves and cypress trees facing the steep peak of Tuscany's Monti Pisani, just over three miles from the historic town of Lucca. Originally a nineteenth-century hunting lodge, Albergo Villa Marta is the property of a young local couple who have poured heart and soul into its restoration and refurbishment. Open for just two years, the Villa Marta is managed by the couple as a charming B&B, with fifteen rooms divided between the villa's two square buildings. The grounds of Villa Marta are meticulously groomed, allowing lazy mornings by the manicured pool to double as horticultural appreciation. There is also a neoclassical chapel at the front of the olive grove used for private ceremonies and events. For the more active guests, brand-new bicycles are available for touring the surrounding area, while bookworms will enjoy the multiple reading nooks complete with comfortable chairs and reading materials dotting the property.

Named after Marta, the patron saint of hotels, the *albergo* pays homage by doing as much as it can to be the ideal hotel. The ultimate goal of the proprietors is to provide their guests with the opportunity to truly relax in an amiable setting. Both Andrea and Alessia Martinelli are involved in every aspect of the hotel's management, from waiting tables at dinner to watering the extra-large terra-cotta flower pots around the villa's exterior. Both Andrea and Alessia strive to keep the villa fresh and reflective of the local area by employing a chef native to the area and showcasing local artists on a revolving three-month schedule. Painting courses are offered at the villa, as are wine tastings. Wholly invested in his hotel and its success, Andrea is eager to please, regularly seeking out the opinions of his guests and inviting suggestions for improving their experience at the villa. His open and communicative attitude is a refreshingly humble approach among today's hotel managers.

The hotel serves a decadent breakfast spread as well as a light lunch and a delicious, substantial dinner that is the true highlight of the villa's amenities. Botton d'Oro, the hotel's restaurant, is Andrea's pride, evident through his beaming presentation of hearty, local cuisine and excellent wine pairings. A large plate teeming with antipasti treats like *crostini*, freshly cured meats and cheeses, and the peppery olives from the villa's groves sets the tone, followed by entrées like creamy gnocchi and buttered lamb shank. The dessert menu is equally ample, though given the robust nature of the earlier dishes it is difficult to muster up an appetite. Chiara, the chef, is affable and ambitious and always open to critiques from the guests—very much like Andrea and Alessia. Cooking classes with Chiara are also available with prior reservation.

The imperial architecture of Villa Marta's front entrance

ABOVE *The well-manicured pool landscape at Albergo Villa Marta*

OPPOSITE *View of the former hunting lodge from the olive groves*

A central location—just one hour from Florence, an hour and a half to Siena, and thirty minutes to the Tuscan coast—makes Albergo Villa Marta an easy and comfortable home base for touring the area. However, it may be a challenge to steer yourself away from the hotel's lulling tranquility. Fortunately, the nearby historic town of Lucca, with its museums, fine restaurants, and various social events, will satiate even the most restless, culture-seeking vacationers. Complimentary bikes offer a pleasant active diversion and are comfortable enough for the three-mile trip to Lucca.

THE ROOMS

The villa's eleven rooms are decorated in a traditional style and painted in pastel hues that reflect those found in the local landscape. Furnished with simple wooden pieces and classic country floral fabrics, the rooms' charms are found through the careful attention paid to the specific color schemes. Woven sisal carpets add a comfortable, homey touch, and are particularly cozy for wet feet straight from the pool. The double deluxe room done in a cream palette with a painted ceiling is one of the more attractive at the villa. The better rooms are those on the third floor of the main villa or the second floor of the second, smaller building. The higher the room, the better the view of the hillside olive grove, surrounding gardens, and towering Pisani mountains. All rooms are air-conditioned and have satellite TV and mini-bars.

CLOCKWISE FROM TOP LEFT
*An antique scale on display;
the modest country style in
the guestrooms; the daily
breakfast spread, all fresh
and locally grown*

OPPOSITE *Terra-cotta floors
and beamed ceilings keep the
Villa rooted in its origins*

ABOVE *The simple elegance of the hotel's lobby* | OPPOSITE *A glass of wine is always available at the Albergo Villa Marta*

VILLA CABBIAVOLI

CASTELFIORENTINO, TOSCANA

*L*OCATING the private Villa Cabbiavoli is a challenge. Secluded in a small hamlet in the Chianti valley, not far from Siena, the villa is a true hideaway. Only after winding past mowed fields and climbing up steep, unmarked forested roads does the gated entrance to Villa Cabbiavoli reveal its stone pillars and charming driveway lined with potted geraniums. Emerging from the car to face the remarkable layout of the estate's three separate historical structures is the reward. The estate has both a magnificent twelfth-century tower and a thirteenth-century chapel on the property, and the elegant main villa dates back to the early thirteenth century, when it was used as a noble family's castle and fort. A sumptuous mixture of three typically Tuscan architectural relics, the initial stunning view of the estate is enhanced by the incredible garden and flowers surrounding the buildings. An explosion of purple bougainvillea erupts from the side of the chapel, creating a wondrous canopied pathway to the dining terrace, and an immense magnolia tree dominates the center lawn.

The pool sits just below the front lawn on its own level overlooking the vineyards, olive groves, yellow fields, and forests. The views from Villa Cabbiavoli are, simply put, breathtaking. And the best part is that there are so many exceptional vantage points from which to enjoy them. The perspective from the top of the tower is a unique highlight with 360-degree views of the

property, the owner's surrounding *agriturismo* (farmland open for tourist visits), and, if you crane your neck, the tower of the historic Tuscan town San Gimignano. Deck chairs sit folded along the wall, tempting the visitor into staying longer. The chapel has a small altar and a statue of Christ with two rows of pews. Behind the chapel is a small sun porch with stairs leading up to a rooftop terrace complete with a coffee table and chairs ideal for sunset viewings. Well suited for families, the villa also has a Ping-Pong table out on the patio, a fusbol table on the sun porch, and multiple televisions with DVD players.

The downstairs interiors of the Villa Cabbiavoli exhibit impeccable taste. The entry room is an ornamented ode to hunting—a widely practiced passion in Tuscany. Wild boar tusks and skulls and other unidentifiable trophies adorn the walls of the front room, and forest-themed furniture and lamps help create a cozy atmosphere. The traditional-style dining room features large oil paintings and an elegant mahogany table with antique candelabras. The small library off the living room offers a quiet place to read, with antique framed maps and built-in bookshelves. A writer's desk with Ethernet connection and a small black marble fireplace smooth the transition for the occasional foray into work. The room most marked by the villa's noble past, however, is the living room, with custom details and fine antiques; a white Boullion fringe with tassel

The family Cabbiavoli's thirteenth-century chapel

detail on the two velvet Knoll sofas is particularly appealing, as is the striking mix of pink and gold Carerra marble in the fireplace, which casts a warm tone over the room. High-quality fabrics on the wingback chairs and oil paintings mixed with family portraits complete the room, giving it the perfect sense of being both well done and well worn.

Villa Cabbiavoli's secluded location in the heart of the Chianti valley ensures ample privacy. Just thirty minutes from Florence, the villa is also a perfect home base for touring Tuscany's vast wine country and gastronomic delights. In fact, it was Villa Cabbiavoli that gave rise to the red wine Chianti Putto Fattoria di Cabbiavoli, produced from Sangiovese and Cannaiolo grapes. A well-respected extra-virgin olive oil is also made on the family's neighboring *agriturismo* operation. The caretaker Maria is also available to cook meals upon request and offers a charming perspective into the ways of the local lifestyle with her amiable and eager personality and myriad of stories.

THE ROOMS

The villa has six bedrooms, all traditionally decorated and referred to by their color schemes. The upstairs rooms have large shuttered windows that open out to the yard and magnolia tree below. They provide long, sweeping views of the multi-colored hillside and allow the occasional cool breeze to filter in, carrying the floral scents from below. The blue room has a painted ceiling depicting the sky, while the yellow room has a long mahogany armoire. The ground-floor bedroom has whimsical gold cherubs above the bed and a light-green silk woven bed cover, giving the room an elegant appeal. The beauty of the villa's interiors is in their detailed and careful decoration. Hours can be spent noting the smaller decorative elements present in each room and marveling at the wonderful personal details like family portraits, valuable heirlooms, and custom furnishings. Guests can't help but feel encouraged to dream about moving in permanently and becoming a part of the Cabbiavoli family.

ABOVE *Custom tassel detailing on the sofa in the living room (left); angelic accents in the master bedroom (right)*

OPPOSITE *The exquisite décor of the living room*

ABOVE *The master's study with its collection of antique globes* | OPPOSITE, CLOCKWISE FROM TOP LEFT *The Villa's embellished facade; the roof terrace complete with sitting area; the front yard's magnificent magnolia tree; the painted ceiling of the blue room*

LA BANDITA

BRAND new in 2007, La Bandita is the Tuscan castle in the sky of owner John Voightmann and his wife, Ondine. Trading in his successful music-industry career to build and run an inn in Tuscany's picture-perfect Val D'Orcia area, Voightmann has effectively imported his American Dream. On the top of a large hill, alongside a sheep farm and surrounded by land belonging to UNESCO (meaning the land will forever remain undeveloped), La Bandita presents a breathtaking panoramic view as well as the ultimate hideaway location. The driveway to La Bandita is a long, winding gravel path, unmarked off the main road. It jostles and bumps you as you climb and then climb some more, prompting prayers that your rental car will survive the trip. Yet as soon as you plateau and park, the sweet, cool breeze and 360-degree view of Tuscany's beloved rolling hills are like a tonic to the now-forgotten discomfort of the drive.

Voightmann greets his road-weary guests with a handshake and an offer of Campari and soda, instantly communicating the intended casual and relaxed mood of La Bandita. The inn is meant to feel like a friend's home, and though the service and amenities most likely outdo those of your acquaintances, the overall sentiment is that you are among friends and encouraged to act accordingly. Comprised of two squat stone farmhouses, one big, one small, the exterior of La Bandita presents quite modestly, but nothing

could be further from the truth. Stepping into the main house's front room is like having the elevator door open into a contemporary loft in Tribeca. The open design is done all in white, save for the back wall, which is painted a warm honey color. The singular color effectively draws out the room's many wooden window and door frames, and pleasantly offsets the kitchen's steel countertop and metallic ceiling lamps. The effect is a distinct departure from the typical Tuscan farmhouse interior and wholly refreshing. Incorporated into the décor are the owners' two passions: music and travel. The centerpiece of the room is a custom couch and table hybrid, which showcases an impressive vinyl collection and record player. The connecting sitting room and library features a large sectional couch surrounded by bookshelves brimming with travel guides, all organized by region. The hotel is very much the couple's home, though they do stay off property when the inn is at capacit. John's dropdown desk is right in the library, and Ondine can often be found typing at the kitchen table.

Located just south of Siena near Pienza and midway between Rome and Florence, La Bandita is an ideal location from which to explore the beauty and gastronomical bounty of Tuscany as well as plan day trips to the big cities. Both John and Ondine are quick with good suggestions for activities and touring sites, and John is quickly becoming an excellent event planner. The inn

Infinite pleasure at the pool at La Bandita

offers full family-style dining for guests twice a week. The chef prepares local Tuscan fare, and John and Ondine preselect complementary local wines. Dinner is usually served under the outdoor terra-cotta-framed pergola, where pink sunsets provide the backdrop. As at most Italian hotels, breakfast is served on portable trays left waiting outside your room. Other snacks, drinks, and a never-ending supply of espresso are available for the taking. The inn's infinity pool is just fifty yards beyond the house on the only plot of land on which Voightmann could obtain permission from the Italian bureaucracy to build. Luckily for his guests, it is the ideal spot to lounge and watch the water lap endlessly toward the patchwork yellow-and-brown hills. Another favored pastime at La Bandita is watching the neighbors: the sheep. Two white-backed director's chairs sit atop a small molehill perfectly set up for viewing the sheep's twice-daily trips down toward the water hole. Life at La Bandita is perhaps best encapsulated by the sheep's daily routine, simple and hassle-free. Absent of pretense and luxuriously casual, La Bandita has what most small inns are after: authenticity and individualism.

THE ROOMS

The eight rooms at La Bandita are simple and quirky yet quite comfortable. The mission behind the interiors of La Bandita was to take the typical Tuscan materials—terra-cotta, stone, cement-based fresco paint—and employ them in an unusual way. The terra-cotta canopy bed-frames are an attractive original design by the owners, and the floors are a smooth white stone–

which Ondine says was shocking to the Italians who laid them. The few colored walls were painted using the same wet cement mixed with paint used for frescoes. This ensures that the color is actually a part of the wall. The effect is as dramatic as it is curious. Funky furnishings like Kelly green fold-down desks, white plush down comforters, and thick cushioned chaise longues keep the rooms feeling whimsical as well as practical. The walls of the bathroom's free-standing rain shower are painted a deep aqua, and the showerhead is a cube shape equipped with its own light, which when turned on turns the shower into a streaming spotlight. All of this can be vaingloriously witnessed from the bathroom's vertical mirror, hung at the flattering angle favored by women's dressing rooms.

Ondine, a travel writer, visits and stays at countless hotels around the world, which is perhaps why La Bandita's bed linens, bath products, and robes are the best on the market. The linens are by Busatti, the skin-care products by Eau D'Italie, pharmacy of Santa Maria Novella and Chianti Cashmere Goat Farm, and the robes are from Boca Terry—which the couple first spotted at the Raleigh hotel in Miami. The bulk of the rooms are located in the main house, while the secondary farmhouse, known as the pig sty, has one and a half bedrooms and an en-suite kitchen—ideal for a couple with small children. The property can also be rented exclusively by the day or by the week and sleeps up to sixteen people. The rental comes with daily maid service, concierge, a welcome basket of groceries, and the services of a private chef upon request.

*The second floor sitting
room's quiet simplicity
(left); Voightmann's
prized possessions*

ABOVE *Terra-cotta modern employed at La Bandita*

OPPOSITE *A reflection of the sunset in the front door of La Bandita*

CLOCKWISE FROM TOP LEFT
*The owner's original terra
cotta bed frame design in
the guestrooms; stylish bath
products in the bathroom of
the pig-sty suite; only the
finest robes and soaps will do
for the guests at La Bandita*

OPPOSITE
The spotlighted shower

IL FALCONIERE

MOST definitely under the Tuscan sun (Frances Mayes lives close by and is a friend of the owners, Riccardo and Silvia Baracchi), Il Falconiere lies on the hill slightly below and across from Cortona, Italy's famed ancient Etruscan hillside town. A typical Tuscan estate, it dates back to the seventeenth century and was once the home of the renowned poet Antonio Guadagnoli. The property is pleasantly spread out, allowing for a wide variety in room selection and many secret spots from which to enjoy the peaceful splendor of Italy's countryside. With two pools, a Michelin-star restaurant with both indoor and outdoor seating, a chapel, a celebrated cooking school, and a fully operational wine cantina whose grapes come from the vines that line the property, Il Falconiere is a Tuscan hamlet unto itself.

The estate has been in the Baracchi family since 1860, when it operated as a self-sustaining farm focused on wine and olive oil production. In 1989, when the property was left to Riccardo Baracchi, he and his wife, Silvia, decided to open a restaurant in the restored conservatory of the estate. Then in 1993 they decided to add rooms alongside the restaurant, turning the destination restaurant into a hotel and creating, as he calls it, a *piccolo mondo*, or small world. Il Falconiere opened with just nine rooms, and then a few years later came further restoration of the surrounding structures, a new pool, more

rooms, a cooking school run by the very talented Silvia, and a renovated cantina for Riccardo's wine production. In 1997, the elite French hotel group Relais & Chateaux added the now twenty-room property and its restaurant to its prestigious catalog, validating Riccardo's initial vision. Today Riccardo feels that Il Falconiere now has everything it needs to once again exist on its own; when he welcomes his guests, he indeed invites them into a genuine "small world." The view from Il Falconiere is like a dramatic landscape painting, especially when the rolling valley is draped in that warm fuchsia light particular to the Tuscan sunset. Sitting at the hotel's canopy bar sipping a glass of the Baracchi red wine, whose origin, the Sangiovese grape, can be seen growing just off to your left, while admiring the sun's setting colors has a certain cinematic glow to it.

The name *Il Falconiere* comes from Riccardo and Silvia's passion for hunting and the ancient art of falconry. The falcon adorns the estate's wine-bottle label and the hotel's promotional material, but is best appreciated in the flesh. A real, live falcon, cared for by Silvia, lives and breathes on the property. The dominance of the natural world at Il Falconiere is evident through not only the animals (Silvia and Riccardo's big dogs are never far behind them, and guests' pets are welcome), but also by Silvia and Riccardo's dedication to the land,

Country elegance: the Cantina Suite at Il Falconiere

To eat at Il Falconiere's Michelin-starred restaurant, whether for lunch or dinner, is an unforgettable indulgence. It begins with the five-choice bread-selection process, theatrically performed by white-smocked waiters. The homemade olive oil offered alongside quickly tips you off to the purity of the approaching food. To be on a diet here is a crime and an insult to the Roman mantra *Carpe diem*. Moreover, the best part of the whole meal might just be the dessert. While that seems unfair to the delectable fresh raviolini or the juicy slab of fresh meat cut right before you, the glistening merry-go-round tray of sugary temptresses (including a wonderful chocolate and pistachio mousse) that is presented post-meal will both haunt and delight you.

THE ROOMS

The Winery Suite at Il Falconiere has a commanding view of the property, including the vineyards below. The terrace outside the massive suite has two comfortable lounge chairs that silently encourage a private afternoon of reading, as well as a romantic viewing of the epic sunset to follow. The room's interior has a rustic charm, with a large carved-wood bed frame, an antique painted headboard, and tapestry crown canopy. The room's grand size accommodates a full sitting area with a fireplace and television and a gorgeous wooden writer's desk, while the small rectangle windows that line the room frame the views of the surrounding landscape like pictures, keeping the atmosphere cozy and intimate. There is also a back room that doubles as a large walk-in closet and houses the mini-bar, a large armoire, and a small loft with two twin beds. The suite is ideal for a couple with children, though to have it for just one is to feel beyond spoiled.

particularly with regard to the food and the wine that come from it.

Riccardo is passionate about his latest revolutionary enterprise: Prosecco developed from the Sangiovese grape. His eyes lit up as he showed off the cavelike room that houses the bottles, only a thousand of them now in existence, of which maybe only half will survive, and demonstrated the rudimentary hand-turning motion he and his son must apply to each bottle individually in order for the Prosecco to develop properly.

Breakfast is served under the pergola at Il Falconiere

CLOCKWISE FROM TOP LEFT
*Artisanal lamps and head-
boards in the guestrooms; the
custom details in the Cantina
Suite; picture-perfect viewing
from the Cantina Suite*

ABOVE *The cottage suites* | OPPOSITE *The view from the Cantina Suite of vineyards and Tuscany's Monte Amiata in the distance*

VILLA CASTELLETTO

MONTICCHIELLO, TOSCANA

TUCKED back off a rural farm road accessed just before the ancient stone town of Monticchiello in Tuscany's postcard-perfect Val D'Orcia valley is architect Michele Cantatore's seven-bedroom stone farmhouse. Lovingly restored and decorated by Cantatore and his late wife, Emanuela Stramana, Villa Castelletto is over a thousand years old, according to Cantatore. Before the passing of his wife, Signore Cantatore lived on the property year round but now rents out the house for the majority of the year, preferring to stay in a small apartment near his office in Monticchiello; a jovial caretaker and his young son live on the premises, tending to the impressive gardens and pool area. The house is a true testament to the many happy and fruitful years Cantatore and Stramana spent together at the home, and the many decorative treasures on display are in fact mementos, each with its own story. In order to gain total appreciation of the house and its glory it is best to be given a personal tour by Signore Cantatore accompanied by his faithful terriers. Listening to his recounting of how he and his wife came to own the gorgeous, ancient marble sink originally belonging to the Medici family, or how his wife hung her hat on one of the exposed beams in the back entryway and so liked how it looked that she added about twenty more sun hats to cover the room's ceiling, is beyond heartwarming. The kitchen is yet another marvelous glimpse into the

couple's enviable Tuscan existence and a superb enticement for your own. A large oak island is both the preparation center and informal kitchen table. Dried herbs hang from the ceiling rafters, and cast-iron posts decorate the wall above the range stove. A wooden music stand next to the oven holds open recipe books that serve as windows into the kitchen's illustrious past.

The villa's hilltop location affords an expansive view across an oak forest, small local vineyards, and olive groves, and out toward Tuscany's famed Monte Amiata. The gardens below are filled with herbs planted by Stramana, and a myriad of flowers and fruit trees. Because Cantatore and his wife refurbished the house themselves and architectural refurbishment is Cantatore's expertise, the guided tour is also fascinatingly educational. Cantatore deftly explains the procedures that went into restoring the ancient home and points out such beloved historical markers as the eight-hundred-year-old olive tree in the garden and a few original steps from the medieval pilgrimage path from France to Rome known as Via Frangicena. There's even a hidden stone vault where locals would leave milk for passing pilgrim mothers and their children. The most marked beauty of Villa Castelletto is its ivy-covered multi-Roman-arched facade with two separate loggias. Window boxes of red geraniums fill the second-floor arches, and large rosemary bushes line the

The sun-filled Loggia off the master bedroom

ABOVE *The Villa's guesthouse*

OPPOSITE *The ivy-covered exterior of Villa Castalletto*

ground floor, giving the house an old-world feel reminiscent of a time when gardens were the true mark of a home's grandeur.

The property is set around a central courtyard that once housed farm animals. Now it is the site for idyllic Italian meals served al fresco at two round tables on either side of a pear tree with crisscrossing grapevines dangling overhead. Across from the main house is an outdoor portico originally used to store farm equipment and carriages but now transformed into a charming outdoor patio with a pleasant view out to the gardens and forest below. The villa is located between the historic towns of Montepulciano and Pienza, both fantastic for touring and wine tasting, while the nearby walled town of Monticchiello is an easy five-minute drive and features a few shops and quaint local restaurants—including La Porta whose Tuscan fare is reliable and delightful.

THE ROOMS

The rooms of Villa Castelletto were carefully decorated by Stramana, who found most of the furniture from local antique markets in nearby Montepulciano. However, various items, like the bed in the master bedroom, are courtesy of a trip to Venice or from the couple's earlier life in Africa. The house is fully winterized and has two large fireplaces on both the first and second floors. The two double rooms on the second floor in the main house are painted a warm Tuscan gold and feature muslin bedcovers and canopy beds. There is a bathroom for each bedroom, making the villa a comfortable group rental as well. There is also a separate guesthouse, with a small living room and freshly appointed bedroom and bathroom, ideal for a couple with a small child.

CLOCKWISE FROM TOP LEFT
Treasured artifacts on display; the country kitchen; the Tuscan library

OPPOSITE *The farmhouse-style guestroom complete with fireplace*

CASTELLO DI VICARELLO

POGGI DEL SASSO, TOSCANA

*I*F simply locating this isolated second-century Roman castle feels triumphant, then spending a few days here is nothing short of glorious. Castello di Vicarello, in Tuscany's coastal Maremma area, is indeed special, magnificent, and, most certainly, removed. Returning to Castello di Vicarello after a day of wine tasting in Montepulciano or swimming at the beach is a distinct privilege. Not only is the ancient castle breathtakingly beautiful, with manicured grounds and flowers and herbs fragrantly abloom, but there's also a palpable warmth that emanates from the property. Perhaps it's the castle's rich history, or perhaps it is the secluded setting amid fields and forest, but more likely it is the castle's personable owners, Aurora and Carlo Baccheschi Berti, and their three delightful teenage sons.

The Baccheschi Berti family's influence is apparent everywhere at Castello di Vicarello. From the careful restoration by Carlo to the very personal interior decoration by Aurora to the obvious reality that half of the castle is in fact the family's home, to be a guest at Castello di Vicarello is to be welcomed into the lives of the people who run it. In the family for almost thirty years, the castle took on a whole new character after Carlo retired from his successful career in the film business. Together with Aurora, he converted and restored the half of the castle they would not occupy themselves into four guest

rooms, then refurbished the two tangential structures into a one-bedroom suite and a two-bedroom cottage.

For Carlo, each guest is a potential friend, and he enjoys charming guests with extra glasses of his delicious private-label Cabernet or, if he's feeling particularly amiable, leading them up to the grass-covered rooftop terrace to enjoy a most amazingly clear and intimate view of the night sky and Milky Way. What makes staying at Castello di Vicarello so special is the owners' unwavering sincerity. The gregarious hosts share their passion for the castle and the land with the guests by creating a convivial and inclusive atmosphere. Don't be surprised if Aurora waves you into the kitchen to watch her bake the evening's dessert or, if having noted your interest in wine, Carlo invites you down to tour his vineyards and bring back wine for dinner.

The property's extensive grounds feature two custom-designed pools—one a marble infinity pool overlooking the valley and, on a clear day, the sea, and the second a secluded garden pool with teak deck surrounded by lavender bushes and olive trees. Freshly mowed lawns are framed by stunning gardens that feature bushes of roses, lavender, and jasmine plus rows of lemon, olive, and pear trees. Castello di Vicarello is open year round, and its warm, country Tuscan interiors complete with stone fireplaces promise cozy winter nights. During the autumn hunting

Morning warmth: the breakfast room at Castello di Vicarello

season, Carlo also runs a nearby hunting lodge, Valle di Buraino, twenty minutes from the castle. On this separate 780-acre property, Carlo organizes wild-boar-hunting expeditions for groups in the traditional Italian style, which entails a full meal and award ceremony at the end of the day.

With Aurora in the kitchen and Carlo out in the vineyards, the homemade meals consist of homegrown fruits, vegetables, and herbs paired with delicious local cheeses, fish, and meats. Castello di Vicarello is spoiled by its proximity to both fresh game and fresh fish by being only an hour away from the sea. Guests are also treated to the castle's own extra-virgin olive oil and organic wine produced on the estate. Cooking lessons with Aurora and wine tastings with Carlo are available on request. Both lunch and dinner are served in the idyllic stone courtyard between the castle's two wings. Seating options include a long communal oak table right off the Baccheschi Bertis' living room or the smaller circular table tucked in the corner near the arched entrance. Both tables enjoy the traditional Tuscan canopy of grapevines.

With plans to expand and to add on a small spa and yoga studio, Castello di Vicarello may not stay hidden forever. Fortunately, though, Carlo and Aurora are permanent fixtures.

THE ROOMS

The six rooms at Castello di Vicarello are eclectically decorated, demonstrating the personal taste and past lives of Aurora. Many of the furnishings, including a stately four-poster mahogany bed, hail from Indonesia. Having spent eighteen years there, Aurora has amassed a vast collection of Indonesian and Balinese furniture and fabrics. She even imported design elements like bamboo wall dividers for the en-suite bathroom in Chiesina, the two-bedroom cottage, and an

ornate daybed for Carlo's sitting room off the courtyard. The rooms at Castello di Vicarello are varied and should be chosen based on the level of privacy desired. The four guest rooms are located right across the narrow stone courtyard from the family's quarters, ensuring an up-close and personal look at the family's comings and goings, including Aurora's delicious cooking, of which guests are invited to partake. The separate structures, Villa Sasso and Villa Chiesina, are considerably more removed from the family and can be rented on a weekly basis. The bedroom at Villa Sasso is painted a rich Tuscan red and has two large bay windows facing the rolling hills and on a spectacularly clear day can offer a glimpse of the sea. The bathroom is deliciously spacious with a terry cloth chaise lounge and stone shower. The middle sitting room, though, is the true highlight with an entire wall of sliding glass doors facing out to the view. When all the doors are pulled open, the constant breeze will cause the linen curtains to billow and the scent of jasmine to fill the room. Villa Chiesina, on the other hand, is a complete house with two large bedrooms and its own kitchen and private dining terrace. The second-floor bedroom offers a commanding view of the hills and distant sea and feels wonderfully refreshing with its neutral and cream color scheme. Lovingly decorated by Aurora, each room at Vicarello is differentiated by a unique touch, such as the Indonesian daybed in the second-floor guest room or the stone-laid fireplace and cozy sitting area in the duplex room. The custom details in the rooms allow the visitor to truly feel as though he or she is a personal guest in Carlo and Aurora's home. To ensure booking a room that suits your tastes, it is best to confer first with Aurora or Carlo. The entire property is also available for exclusive rental upon request.

The ancient castle's courtyard at dusk

CLOCKWISE FROM TOP LEFT
*The en suite bathroom of the
Sasso Suite; the Sasso Suite's
airy sitting room; a purple
artichoke decorates the living
room of the main guesthouse*

OPPOSITE *Villa Sasso's inviting bedroom*

ABOVE *View of the castle from the garden pool* | OPPOSITE *Worthy of an evening stroll: the grounds of Castello di Vicarello*

VILLA MANGIACANE

ENTERING the imperial front gate flanked by massive stone pillars featuring imposing stone dog sculptures is to travel back in time to an era when villas were designed to intimidate as much as impress.

Just twenty minutes outside of Florence, Villa Mangiacane sits proudly on the top of a vineyard-laden hill, directly facing Brunelleschi's dome. The dome can be seen perfectly through a keyholelike view that has been cut straight through the forest. Villa Mangiacane's original inhabitant, Nicolo Macchiavelli, commissioned the deforestation during his imposed exile from Florence during the Medici family rule. A grand sixteenth-century villa that is rumored to have been partly designed by Michelangelo, Villa Mangiacane was sold by the Machiavelli family in 1645 to the noble Marcheis Mazzei family. It remained in their family until 2000 when South African entrepreneur and wine lover Glynn Cohen bought it and rescued it from neglect. With the initial intent of keeping the villa for private use only, Cohen poured all his time and resources into refurbishing and reinstating the villa's original splendor. Villa Mangiacane (meaning "the dog that eats") has also returned to its original wine-producing roots. In 2000 Cohen hired Alberto Antonini, formerly of Antinori wine, to be the lead wine maker in charge of revitalizing the villa's original viticulture, which dates back five hundred years. Today

it bottles an impressive Villa Mangiacane Chianti Classico and Chianti Classico Riserva. Once Cohen had restored the main villa, filling its main rooms with gorgeous antiques and fabrics and its eight deluxe bedrooms with magnificent elements like sterling silver bed frames imported from India, he recognized the potential for a small hotel and opened Villa Mangiacane to the public, advertising its existence simply through word of mouth. More recent is the restoration of the Tuscan farmhouse behind the main villa, now known as Villa Vignetta , which includes eighteen decadent suites, some with private lap pools.

The defining characteristic of Villa Mangiacane as a hotel is its diverse styles. Gliding between the desire to preserve and honor the villa's prestigious Italian heritage while incorporating a modern, funky design aesthetic and simultaneously paying homage to the owner's South African roots, Villa Mangiacane's aesthetic is wholly distinctive. The vying themes can be seen most clearly through its two pools. The pool by the Villa Vignetta is a brand-new infinity-edge pool (the standard among Italy's more recent hotels), while the cabana tents and bright white leather pool bar feel as though they came right out of Africa. The pool at the main villa, on the other hand, is the original pool of the property and boasts a proud Machiavellian stone lion fountain at its head. Iron chaise longues and a quaint vine-covered pergola dining area evoke an English garden aesthetic. The

The magnificent sterling silver bed in Villa Mangiacane's deluxe room

overall sentiment is of an old-world sanctuary. The spa is another demonstration of the fusion between traditional Italian elements and the distinctively varied style of Villa Mangiacane. The spa is located in the basement of the main villa, and its three massage trooms, indoor pool, sauna, steam bath, and a small weight room are tucked in right alongside the villa's large wine barrels and storage vault. The waiting area of the spa features a large white couch that faces poster-sized black-and-white nude portraits taken of women all over the villa's grounds and a large picture window showcasing the temperature-controlled wine vault. Whether all these whimsical contradictions can be attributed to Cohen or to his team of designers, the contradictions they pose are fascinating. In a nod to Cohen's devotion to his home continent, Zimbabwean sculptures dot the front lawn of the main villa; these are for sale in an effort to promote Zimbabwean art to the world.

The main activity at Villa Mangiacane is lounging. With two pools, two lunch spots, an elegant dining room, spa, and an enormous loggia with a view of Florence where breakfast is served, it is the perfect place to unwind. Should you require more activity, Florence and Siena are quick drives, and the many tempting vineyards of the Chianti region surround you.

THE ROOMS

The twenty-six rooms and suites at Villa Mangiacane come in a dramatic variety and differ quite notably from one another. The rooms are split between two main structures: the newer Villa Vignetta, which houses nineteen suites of varying levels, and the refurbished main villa, which holds eight well-appointed suites. The deluxe rooms in the Villa Vignetta along with the junior suites are bound to awe guests with their fanciful design, contemporary décor, and undeniable decadence. Although each room is decorated in its own unique style—one is done entirely in black and white complete with zebra upholstery—consistency is found through magnificent beds and linens. The bed in room number 33 on the second floor of Villa Vignetta featured a light tan leather bed frame, and its mattress and pillows were filled with possibly all the goose-down feathers to be found in Italy. Forcing oneself out of bed in the morning will not be easy, but luckily the all-glass shower or leather-lined circular Jacuzzi stocked with fresh-smelling Italian bath products made by Zinzare make for an easy transition to the day ahead. The décor in the main villa is decidedly more traditional and referential to the villa's sixteenth century past. Gorgeous silk fabrics adorn the furniture in the downstairs sitting rooms and set the stage for the grandness of the guest rooms.

The ground floor deluxe room in the main villa is one of the smaller rooms in the main villa though renowned among visitors. The light, whether it be morning or afternoon, emphasizes the room's remarkable beauty and simplicity. Painted a soft yellow and dominated by its stunning sterling silver four-poster bed, the room has an innocence to it, as if it came directly from a watercolor illustration found in a Victorian children's book. Perhaps it's the mixture of yellow walls, blue-and-white porcelain lamps, gauzy white bed curtains, and orchids that give the room its joyful, idyllic quality. More likely it's the incredible bed. The terrace suites, also located on the second floor of the main villa, are particularly attractive with their high ceilings, seventeenth-century fabrics and furnishings, and most of all, their sweeping views of the vineyards and Florence off in the distance. Whether you choose to stay in the more modern Villa Vignetta or the traditional main villa, the opulence and custom interior design of your room is assured, though if a view is a prerequisite, then it is best to book a room in the main villa facing out to the vineyards.

CLOCKWISE FROM TOP LEFT
*Floating floral details; high
concept design patterns in the
suites of the Villa Vignetta;
the elegant interior of the
deluxe ground-floor room*

ABOVE *Opulent furnishings in the villa's living room (left); Macchiavelli's view from the Villa's loggia (right)*

OPPOSITE *The peach colored facade of Villa Mangiacane*

HOTEL LUNGARNO

PROMINENTLY positioned on the south shore of Florence's Arno River, Hotel Lungarno is hardly a hideaway. However, its stylish and classic rooms are remarkably fresh and comfortable, and provide a modern sophistication that makes a wonderful contrast to a city so richly steeped in historical elegance. A polished, contemporary look characterizes this flagship hotel of the Ferragamo family's Lungarno hotels group. The wall-length picture windows of the lobby, with direct views of the Arno just above the water line, give the feeling of being on a cruise ship, and rows of white couches, large glass vases of fresh agapanthus, and gleaming mahogany coffee tables confirm the yacht-inspired design. The spiral staircase, antique brass elevator, and special stone-walled bell-tower suite keep the hotel feeling rooted to Florence.

Signature white pillows with a spunky navy blue fringe trim add a playful tone to the multiple couches, chairs and even the traditional bar furniture in the downstairs lobby. Complimentary wireless service all over the hotel means guests are often seen happily lounging on the couches with their laptops or at the iron café tables on the small outdoor terrace. With the number of American students and their visiting parents ever increasing, Florentine hotels have responded by adding modern amenities, English-speaking staff, and full-service concierges. Hotel Lungarno has gone a step further by offering a signature trendy

The adorned walls of Hotel Lungarno's San Jacopo restaurant

restaurant, with a separate street entrance whose nightly young and sophisticated crowd keeps the hotel feeling vibrant and hip. The exceptional cuisine and chic décor have made it a popular and exclusive dinner option among fashionable Florentines. The walls of Hotel Lungarno also double as a modern art gallery, showcasing contemporary artists' work and various fashion sketches that subtly remind guests of who owns the hotel. The hotel's ideal location on the quieter Boboli Gardens side of the Arno River, fronting the actual river (*Lungarno* translates into "along the Arno") and less than a hundred feet from the Ponte Vecchio, make visiting Florence's many sites exceptionally easy. However, the best part of staying at Hotel Lungarno is returning after a long day of touring and indulging in the hotel's spectacular view by ordering a drink on the terrace or simply gazing out the window from your riverfront room.

THE ROOMS

The décor of the hotel's seventy three rooms is reminiscent of a smartly tailored, little boy's sailor suit: crisp white linens, cream headboards with navy ribbon, white bow detailing on the chairs, and light blue walls. The beds are full mattresses with fluffy down pillows and thin quilted duvets. The neatness of the rooms makes them especially welcoming after a long day of crowds,

museums, and ancient city grit. The furnishings include elegant antique writer's desks, comfortable velvet couches, and classic floor-length ribbon-piped drapes. (If you like the furnishings, they can be purchased at the Lungarno home furnishings store underneath its sister property across the river, Lungarno Suites. Even the soft gray fabric of the restaurant's seating and the leather-topped wooden desks can be bought and shipped home.) The rooms on the sixth and seventh floors offer the best sweeping views of the city, whose red roofs glisten and then sparkle with the day's changing light. The sixth-floor rooms with terraces are a worthwhile indulgence and with table and chairs allow for private al fresco dining. The terrace off room 654 stares directly at Florence's emblematic Brunelleschi's dome and, to the right, provides a bird's-eye view of the Ponte Vecchio. Breakfast on the terrace allows for a dramatic sunrise view of the Arno valley and its epic city and is only surpassed by the sunset's extraordinary slideshow of Florence's ancient skyline.

The tailored approach in the lobby and rooms at Hotel Lungarno

ABOVE *The enviable terrace view of Room 654* | OPPOSITE *The tucked-in approach in the guestrooms*

TORRE DI BELLOSGUARDO

FIRENZE, TOSCANA

*S*ECLUDED in the hills just above Florence and surrounded by botanical gardens, Torre di Bellosguardo is luxuriously private. The hotel is housed in a historic sixteenth-century villa attached to a fourteenth-century tower, intimidating in both its imposing size and in its remarkable beauty. The castle is set on the same hill where Hawthorne wrote *The Marble Fawn* and commands one of the most incredible views of the city, perfectly framed by neatly pruned hedges and gardens.

The hotel's medieval stone facade has thick ivy covering the left side and an attractive garden planted just in front with bushes of lavender, roses, and agapanthus. The main door is made of glass and is thus surprisingly modern, but as soon as it slides back to reveal the spectacularly sized front room, complete with frescoed ceilings and custom moldings, the antique aesthetic of the hotel is confirmed. The reception desk sits dwarfed in a corner, justly forcing the guest's attention to the room's remarkable dimensions, rich draperies, and Oriental rugs. The already compelling desire to explore the massive villa's interior is heightened when you hear a shrill, high-pitched shriek. The porter, accustomed to guests' curiosity, leads you straight back to the immense conservatory known as the *limonaia*, the villa's former lemon tree solarium. There, perched on a simple iron stand, is a large and bellicose parakeet. The *limonaia* is a sunshine-filled

Ancient beauty: the staircase at Torre di Bellosguardo

room with wicker furniture and a canopied daybed ideal for reading—depending on your ability to tune out the chirping.

The preserved interiors of Torre di Bellosguardo allow for effortless imaginings of the noble lifestyle during the Medici family's reign in Florence. Originally the home of Dante's dear friend, the poet Guido Cavalcanti, the villa was built in 1200 as his family home and hunting lodge. Subsequent owners embellished the home, adding frescoes and sculptures including the impressive *Charity* in the entrance done by famed sculptor Francesco Francavilla. The tall arched ceilings, mammoth-sized salon rooms, stone columns, and simple antique furnishings keep all signs of modernity at bay. An antique wood-encased elevator is the only sign of refurbishment since the eighteenth century and while striking, is the clear second choice for transport upstairs or down. The far more alluring choice is the castle's imperial stone staircase. Fantasies of Renaissance balls are not difficult to conjure when floating down these open air stairs into the grand rooms. The hotel's library also doubles as its bar area and features a large flat-screen television, perhaps the sole sign of the twenty-first century.

The hotel's front lawn and pool both offer serenely picturesque views of Florence with Brunelleschi's dome as the proud centerpiece. Mesmerizing at all hours, the view puts on its most miraculous show during the Tuscan sunset. Torre

di Bellosguardo also has a small farm and vegetable garden. Despite having an unparalleled view of the city, Torre di Bellosguardo aptly recognizes that it must also conform somewhat to the expectations of today's travelers, and offers the usual modern amenities; a small gym with treadmill and weights plus an indoor pool and Jacuzzi are available just across from the *limonaia*. Though there is no restaurant at the hotel, the staff will gladly arrange for a causal takeout meal served in your room or the small bar. But that option should be saved for the truly weary given the abundance of delicious options in nearby Florence.

For diversion, the hotel offers cooking classes given by thirty-year veteran chef June Bellamy, who incorporates history into her cooking instruction to give her students a well-rounded sense of the local cuisine. With Florence just a ten-minute ride down the hill, the possibilities for entertaining oneself are endless. And the best part is that no matter how you choose to spend your day, you can rest assured that upon return you will be greeted by one of the most spectacular views and tranquil spots in the Arno valley—the ideal remedy to a hectic day in the city.

THE ROOMS

The sixteen rooms in the large villa vary in size and shape, but all are decorated in the original Florentine style. Due to Torre di Bellosguardo's guarded affinity to its past—it bills itself as a historic residence—the rooms are not particularly lavish, though they are comfortable and well appointed. Heavy brocade fabrics, cotton linens, and simple antique furniture give the rooms a quaint yet refined appeal. The elegant rooms, some with frescoed ceilings, offer another easy glimpse into the villa's noble history. However, not all of the rooms have a view, so it is best to request one when booking. Room 5, on the second floor, features a particularly regal four-poster bed painted a rich emerald green and embossed with gold detailing plus two large windows boasting sparkling city views. The room's heavy wooden door is fitted with an ancient iron lock and key, further demonstrating the villa's historical roots. All the rooms have modern amenities such as LCD televisions, mini-bars, and refurbished bathrooms with showers and bathtubs.

MASSERIA TORRE COCCARO

SAVELETTRI DI FASANO, PUGLIA

At first glance, the main entrance for Masseria Torre Coccaro (sister property to Masseria Torre Maizza, see page 113) appears more Mexican than Italian. An iron fan decorates the top of the front arch's gate, and religious symbols like an embossed sculpture of Saint Mary and the cross adorn the facade. These symbols, along with the mulberry tree alongside the gate, are actually universal signs of welcome to pilgrims. Almost every communal farm, or *masseria*, in the area has a mulberry tree at the entrance. Bright-pink bougainvillea blooms across the right side of the entrance's white grotto wall, creating a dramatic contrast. The driveway is a dusty gravel that seems to have been there for centuries; the doors leading into the limestone buildings are stained a dark red. The front courtyard has an ancient appeal, with the external staircase leading up to the tower on the right and a stunning eighteenth-century chapel with rose-colored facade on the left.

Where Torre Maizza is polished and glamorous, Torre Coccaro is rustic and charming. The attitude is casual and very family-oriented, with lots of open-air space, multiple sitting and game rooms, and a horde of mountain bikes in every size. In the front courtyard, slightly crude yet enticing seating areas rise out of the limestone ruins of the *masseria*'s original foundation. The restaurant, bar, and reception area all flow seamlessly into each other, giving the hotel a laid-back, what's-ours-is-yours feel. The dress code here is decidedly less formal and chic than at Torre Maizza; here the hosts and their guests prefer to focus on comfort and relaxation. Torre Coccaro's Aveda spa is larger than Torre Maizza's, and within its grotto walls you will find, in addition to beauty treatment rooms, an indoor pool, a Jacuzzi, and a small fitness room.

An evening at Torre Coccaro begins with a cocktail enjoyed sitting on one of the courtyard's carved-out limestone benches made comfortable with thick red cushions and pleasantly lit by sparkling lanterns. Casually dressed guests mingle as they stroll through the sitting rooms and marvel at the fascinating contemporary furnishings like an armchair filled with *orrechiete* pasta or a large nestlike chandelier. Dinner is surprisingly decadent, served either inside the arched-ceiling restaurant, originally the farm's stables, or out on the terrace. Thick formal menus containing a long wine list and multicourse meals seem slightly incongruent to the informal ambience of the hotel. But this is Italy, after all—eating is always a serious affair. Ask the waiter to recommend a good Pugliese wine to complement the homegrown vegetables and fruits and locally procured salamis and olive oil. Breakfast is also an opulent event, with four large banquet tables filled with locally grown fruits, homemade tarts, cakes, and pastries, yogurts, cereals, and everything else one could imagine wanting. The table

The ancient pilgrim's sanctuary: Masseria Torre Coccaro

reserved for beverages features three pitchers of delicious, freshly made smoothies. Torre Coccaro also offers a full-service cooking school where private group lessons can be reserved ahead of time. Heralded as the new Tuscany, Puglia presents an entirely different perspective on rural Italian life. Instead of the iconic rolling hills and stone farmhouses of Tuscany, Puglia is characterized by the flat rocky beaches, olive groves, and the aqua Adriatic Sea. Responsible for producing over two thirds of the country's olive oil, ten percent of its wine, and a good portion of its pasta, eating in Puglia should be a main event.

Both Torre Coccaro and Torre Maizza share access to the attractive Coccaro Beach Club, a ten-minute bike ride from the hotels and the preferred daytime spot for both hotels' guests. The multiple lounge options at the beach club offer comfort for all types of sunbathers. The beach club consists of four parts: the beach, a protected sunbathing deck with a white wooden wall at its back to shield sun bathers from sea breezes, a bungalow-style bar and eating deck, and a separate white cabana for bathrooms and changing rooms. The beach club restaurant serves sushi in an open-air design complete with a large white semicircular bar. The restaurant's walls are covered with photographs of famous boats and sailors (including President John F. Kennedy on his boat in Cape Cod), and two flat-screen televisions showing recent yacht races hang behind the bar. The jolly owner, Vittorio Muolo, a regular at the beach club bar, is happy to discuss his passion for sailing and boats and will make the wise push for getting you out on the hotel's yacht.

The other lounging option is back at Torre Coccaro's pool, another oasis in and of itself. The laguna design includes a hard sand and cement floor and a lapping water's edge. The pool provides a calming atmosphere and makes a nice alternative to the busier beach club. The palm tree umbrellas and daybed-sized deck chairs, complete with triangular pillows, make lounging poolside very comfortable. The large stone pool bar serves lunch and drinks throughout the day.

The beauty of Torre Coccaro and Torre Maizza is that guests are able to choose where to stay depending on their individual travel style, yet they still have the opportunity to experience the other hotel's amenities. The result is the best of both contrasting worlds.

THE ROOMS

The thirty-seven rooms at Torre Coccaro are spread out all over the immense property, some as far as a third of a mile away from the main building. The best rooms are the two fascinating grotto suites below the chapel and the porch deluxe rooms by the pool. Room 6 is the largest grotto suite, with its own private courtyard with lemon trees, a lap pool, an outdoor sitting area, a hammock, and lounge chairs. The interior walls alternate between the limestone grotto of the church above and bedrock stones stacked up to reinforce the foundation. The furniture is modest but comfortably done. The bed, tucked into its own little alcove, has linen sheets and down pillows. The bathroom's mahogany-and-marble tub is especially attractive, nestled into the cavelike stone space and well appointed with olive-oil soap and bath products. The room is a veritable underground cave and may not be for everyone, but with two glass door entrances and a luxurious secluded garden and pool, it makes for a private and unusual hotel stay. The rooms in the tower are more contemporary alternatives, though similarly rustic in furnishings. The regular tower rooms have small balconies that offer views out to the sea, while the deluxe tower rooms offer tiny terraces with chairs and views of the pool or the surrounding olive groves.

*Poolside lounging
at Torre Coccaro*

CLOCKWISE FROM TOP LEFT
*The Suite's bathroom with
mahogany-lined tub; the
private garden and pool area
of the Grotto Suite; the front
sitting room and view out to
the garden*

OPPOSITE *Modern luxury still
reigns with a Tivoli stereo in
the Grotto Suite*

MASSERIA TORRE MAIZZA

SAVELLETRI DI FASANO, PUGLIA

*L*IKE an oasis in the desert, Masseria Torre Maizza and its next-door neighbor and older sister property, Masseria Torre Coccaro (see page 103), are in definite contrast to the area's modest and dusty seaside surroundings. Turning off the highway and into the small fishing village of Savelletri di Fasano offers the thrill of entering uncharted territory. The two hotels are easily spotted by their enormous white towers, which date back to the sixteenth century and were constructed as part of a fortified row of watchtowers built to protect against Turkish invasions. Separated by less than two miles, the two towers were part of Frederick II of Svevia's ingenious sixteenth-century warning system, where the guard of one tower would alert the guard on the next of oncoming invaders by lighting a fire at the top of the tower. The message would then spread down the row like dominos, maintaining a fortified line of protection. Hence Torre Coccaro and Torre Maizza were both *masserie fortificate*, family-run working farms and fortresses, where pilgrims would seek refuge with their animals and families. Owned by the same family, today the two properties share amenities, including a beach club and private yacht, and offer reciprocity at one another's restaurants.

Driving up the freshly paved driveway to Masseria Torre Maizza is a study in contrasts, with a shockingly green, palm-tree-studded golf course on one side and stretches of brown olive groves on the other. From the entrance, the two-year-old hotel exudes glamour. Part ancient *masseria*, part contemporary chic, the hotel's first impression is breezy Mediterranean-island cool.

Although the water is almost a mile away, its influence is apparent in the thatched roof over the restaurant, the teak used around the deck of the pool, the Balinese lounge furniture, and the glossy white exterior of the hotel. The original walls of the *masseria* and the tower house the reception and communal areas, while the rooms are located behind the restaurant and bar in new, uniformly all-white, single-level buildings.

The glamorous style of Torre Maizza is best appreciated in its restaurant and bar. Split between the original white grotto building with high arched ceilings and an outdoor thatched pergola, the restaurant offers both indoor and outdoor dining options. The view from both is of the sleek infinity pool, golf course, and olive groves beyond. The restaurant's interior is light blue and white with a checkerboard marble floor and mahogany banquettes cushioned with square white pillows. The feel is relaxed yet undeniably stylish. The food is also impeccable. Pugliese cuisine of fresh pastas, seafood with capers, and garden vegetables like zucchini and eggplant dominate the menu, and it would be a shame to miss out on the fresh prawns and indigenous crustaceans even if they do require some effort on the part of the diner. The starter of freshly cut

The dapper charm of Torre Maizza's bar

crudités served with the hotel's olive oil for dipping may overshadow the whole meal with its delectable simplicity.

The bar area is also half indoor, half outdoor. The first part is one long narrow archway of a room with mahogany tables and banquettes flush against the wall, with an antique bar at the front and the same checkered black and white marble floor as the restaurant. The look is very 1950s glam; a headscarf and smoking jacket would not seem out of place. French doors lead from the bar to a large enclosed terrace with a row of tables and chairs under a thatched awning at the front and then open lounge seating set back against a long stone wall brilliantly covered in pink bougainvillea. At dusk, small torchlike flames flicker from the many citronella candles that line the hotel's walkways. After-dinner entertainment is provided out on the lounge porch by a keyboard player and vocalist who, in typical Italian fashion, love to see their audience entertained. Above the restaurant is a rooftop terrace, where the sea is in plain view and at night is filled with glowing lanterns, Moroccan pillows, and secret corners.

During the day the hotel's short golf course is a lighthearted diversion with a solid driving range great for practice. Bikes are at guests' disposal for the easy fifteen-minute ride to the hotel's beach club. Jogging trails between the olive groves and tennis courts are nearby. The hotel also owns a private forty-five-foot yacht available for tours and well worth booking ahead of time. An Aveda spa on the property offers a small menu of body treatments and beauty services.

ABOVE *The bougainvillea-covered outdoor lounge*

OPPOSITE *Classic and fresh interiors in the guestrooms*

THE ROOMS

The twenty-eight spacious rooms at Torre Maizza are contemporary and smart-looking with satin sheets and navy coverlets, white leather benches, and mirrored glass doors. Amenities include flat-screen televisions, Tivoli radios, and brand-new marble bathrooms with double vanities. The rooms' color scheme of ivory and navy mixed with dark-stained wood furnishings and chrome fixtures have a clean, tailored appeal. Providing quite a contrast from the land outside, the rooms can feel like a romantic haven, complete with fireplaces. Each room has a small porch overlooking the golf course, and the larger suites have small dipping pools. Set away from the main buildings, the rooms are deliciously private and—thanks to a policy that limits guests to those over age eighteen during the busy summer months—wonderfully quiet.

LA SOMMITA

OSTUNI, an ancient whitewashed village in the southern part of Puglia, the region found in Italy's heel, is a perfect example of Italy's natural and varied bounty. Vaguely Greek, undeniably ancient, and tucked into a mountain a mile from the sea, Ostuni is simply intoxicating. Roaming its narrow cobbled streets, you feel you are somewhere distinct, and the desire to explore is overwhelming. The White City, as it is known, is believed to have been built over two thousand years ago. It encompasses the upper half of the mountain, making for steeper and steeper passageways. As you climb higher, the streets are closed to traffic, which means that an abundance of secret dens and hideaways, like La Sommita, can exist pleasantly secluded.

In order to get to La Sommita you must pre-arrange with the front desk to be met in the town square. Your liaison will then lead you and your car down to a town parking lot, where you can leave your vehicle. The hotel's vehicle is one of the few cars permitted to drive up the otherwise blocked narrow street to La Sommita, and will take you as far as the small square by the hotel's Roman archway entrance where a porter will meet you and carry your bags the last ten feet. The hotel's entrance is at the end of a tight limestone passage that appears to dead-end, but instead leads to a striking sliding glass door just on the left. The door opens into the contemporary-styled reception area, with a tall light-wood desk and

Limestone chic at La Sommita

attractive recessed lighting. The effect is particularly stunning given the hotel's ancient stone exterior. The bar and lounge area is just through the tall arch to the right and is equally compelling. A cavernous tunnel-shaped room with long white couches and a full wall-sized bay window at the very end give the room a locomotive feel. French jazz plays softly from dangling chrome speakers, and the impulse to order a drink from the smooth wooden bar is difficult to ignore. Fortunately, the hotel's spacious design and ancient architecture inspire you to hold off and follow the porter to your room.

Above the bar, on the second floor, is another floor-length lounge with chocolate-brown contemporary-style couches and tall wooden bookcases begging to be plundered. The same melodic accompaniment plays from identical speakers behind the couches, and the back wall is also all glass but with a door leading out to La Sommita's best asset—its verandas. The hotel is decorated sparingly so that the eye travels through the spacious interiors and out to the mountaintop view. The high-altitude location offers a panoramic view of the Adriatic coastline and the seemingly infinite sea. Although the hotel occupies only two floors, its savvy use of its outdoor space, with platform terraces, long balconies, exterior staircases, and multiple outdoor lounge areas, gives it a much larger feel. Sectional teak couches and lounges fill the corners of the three ground-

level porches, while pots of exotic orange desert flowers add a splash of color. At night, floodlights highlight the hotel's multiple levels and cavelike architecture, making an already fabulous stargazing setting feel very chic.

La Sommita shares a wall with an ancient church, and is in fact a whole building within another larger building. Like many ancient cities, Ostuni is believed to have been built on top of another city, so often structures are built around shells of other buildings, preserving the ancient architecture. The effect is as mysterious as it is romantic.

Ostuni has a coastline twelve miles long, and the hotel runs a shuttle (at cost) to the beaches located ten minutes away. The staff will also arrange escorted excursions and horseback-riding tours. The spa, however, is on premises. It offers massages, beauty treatments, and facials as well as its own line of products, Mareminerale, made from local minerals. The hotel's restaurant serves breakfast and dinner, with seating both inside and out. The meals are presented in a sleek, modern way, with heavy black china and square cutlery. Dinner out on the white-walled terrace, under the stars, with light Moroccan music softly playing in the background, is as alluring as it sounds. A two-minute stroll down the narrow street from the hotel, you will find a small local bar alongside a church tucked within

cavelike walls. The modern menu and young clientele provide the perfect glimpse into the compelling contrast that is Ostuni life. The authentic Pugliese restaurant Osteria del Tempo Perso is also just a few minutes' walk down from the hotel. Housed in yet another cave, the restaurants's wall-to-wall antiques and artifacts along with authentic, homemade pastas demonstrate Ostuni's intent to preserve its rich history.

THE ROOMS

The rooms are done in a soothing neutral palette with linen sheets and simple low beds. The terrace rooms have balconies facing out to the water offering panoramic views of Ostuni. The suites are on the bottom level and have walk-in bathrooms and double doors out to enclosed private lounge areas. The suite (pictured here) is a lavishly appointed cavelike room. The walls are inlaid stone, the ceilings are arched, and even the freestanding tub (which looks more like a well) is outlined in plastered stone. Despite the ancient architecture, the rooms are modernly appointed with a large flat-screen television hanging in the bedroom, a glassed-in rain shower, and complimentary Internet hook-up. The rooms at La Sommita offer the ideal combination of ambience and comfort ensuring the guest will vow one day to return.

ABOVE *The cavernous bar (left); night lights of La Sommita*

OPPOSITE *The spacious feel of the suite*

CLOCKWISE FROM TOP LEFT
*The arc globe speaker; one of
the stone terraces that encom-
pass the hotel; the contemporary
design style of La Sommita*

OPPOSITE *The limestone
staircases of La Sommita*

VILLA BECCARIS

VILLA Beccaris is located in Monforte d'Alba, a tiny mountain village in the wine-rich Langhe hills of Piedmont located directly above Piedmont's famous white truffle and wine capital, Alba. The villa's mountaintop location affords sweeping views of the world-renowned vineyards producing grapes made famous by the vintages of the nearby towns, Barolo and Barbaresco. Monforte D'Alba is a small town and close community of local artisans, farmers, wine makers, and small business owners, and at the center of the community lays Villa Beccaris, an eighteenth-century villa turned hotel. Given its prominent location and attractive outdoor entertaining space, Villa Beccaris plays frequent host to local culinary festivals. Being a guest during one of these events is not only gastronomically but also culturally rewarding. Due to the town's small size and dependence on local trade, people are incredibly friendly and eager to discuss their work. It is not uncommon to meet someone and be invited to visit his or her vineyard or restaurant the following day.

Community involvement is at the very heart of Villa Beccaris, and behind many of these fortuitous introductions is Federica, the villa's manager, who, along with her accommodating staff, proudly shares her hometown's vast natural resources and charming inhabitants. The aim to serve and please is what makes the villa such a delightful spot to stay. The genuine smiles of the staff and the thoughtful touches in the rooms—like linen tote bags for the pool, and a Victorian iron pushcart stacked with sun hats and sunscreen—are all testaments to the caring attitude of the Villa Beccaris. Perhaps that is why the overall sentiment at Villa Beccaris seems so definitively feminine. Like a mother tending to her child, the Villa Beccaris caters to the guest's every want and whim. The villa's staff is more than happy to help arrange excursions to the many nearby vineyards or golf courses, or to set up horseback-riding and hot-air-balloon tours. Touring day trips to Torino and Milan are both possible—each is just under two hours away. Villa Beccaris also appears ready-made for hosting a large party, with two permanent gazebos, one outdoors and the other encased in glass overlooking the vineyards below.

The feminine tone is also apparent in the villa's décor and architecture. The building is painted butter yellow with French-blue shutters and matching blue awnings over the doorways. Thin iron fencing and flower boxes protect the property and decorate the balconies above the courtyard. Café-size tables and chairs with small white cushions and a heart motif on the chair backs can be found in the courtyard and on the back lawn. The pool gets the most sun in the afternoon, though its blue-and-white-striped cushioned chaise longues are attractive and comfortable perches throughout the day. The large

A château in mountaintop Italy: Villa Beccaris

Antique charm and comfort in the rooms at Villa Beccaris

iron gazebo just behind the pool provides a shady alternative to the afternoon sun.

The villa serves only breakfast and a light lunch, plus drinks and *aperitivos* throughout the day. The breakfast is served buffet style in the main bar area and then eaten out in the new glass atrium. The view from the atrium is simply spectacular. The glass-and-iron building extends out from the side of the hill and overlooks the scenic valley below, affording a panoramic view of the area's plentiful vineyards. The center of Monforte D'Alba is just a few minutes' walk down the hill from Villa Beccaris, making multiple dinner options very accessible. The crooked cobblestone streets and charming piazza of Monforte D'Alba is one of Villa Beccaris's top assets.

THE ROOMS

The villa has twenty-three rooms in total, including one master suite, eleven deluxe rooms, and eleven classic rooms. The rooms at Villa Beccaris are for the most part soft and romantic, but a few have darker color schemes with black headboards, brass lamps, and heavy, polished furniture. Handsome antique English furniture and a spectacular nineteenth-century gramophone in the front drawing room offset the long silk drapes and cream quilted backboard of the master suite. The deluxe rooms have charming blue-and-white-striped wallpaper in the bathrooms. The traditional and classic aesthetic of the rooms complement the villa's aristocratic roots and prominent location in the village.

CLOCKWISE FROM TOP LEFT
*The sun trolley at the pool;
feminine details in the
guestrooms; the all-glass
dining pavilion*

OPPOSITE *The charming lawn
chairs of Villa Beccaris*

VILLA TIBOLDI

THE resplendent vineyard view from Villa Tiboldi is not easily acquired. Only after surviving the harrowing drive up a steep hill complete with switchbacks and a narrow cliff-side driveway can the dramatic Piedmontese landscape be fully appreciated. The villa is painted pale yellow with light-blue shutters and delicate light-gray iron balconies off the third-floor guest rooms, giving it a pleasantly soft appeal. On top of the square villa is a charming rooftop cupola that fits a small couch and two chairs and offers a 360-degree view of the rolling vineyards surrounding the villa. It makes a delightful spot for enjoying the villa's signature *aperitivo* of Prosecco and fresh strawberries.

The owners, Patrizia and Roberto Damonte, bought the villa eight years ago and spent four years turning it into their dream operation, with Patrizia at the helm of hospitality and Roberto in charge of the restaurant and wine cantina featuring the two brother's local products. Both Patrizia and Roberto make wonderful hosts, always eager to share their passions with their guests. A vineyard tour with Roberto is a crash course in wine making and local history, and if you're lucky includes a fresh snack from the apricot trees alongside the grapevines. Patrizia is an enthusiastic conversationalist, keen to discuss hotel operations and ideas for improving Villa Tiboldi. The two together make a lovely pair and

give Villa Tiboldi a positive, balanced approach to service and authenticity.

The villa's grounds include an outdoor gravel dining terrace, a cliffside lap pool with panoramic views, and a stylish teak deck with wicker umbrellas and cozy cushioned lounge chairs. The hotel's restaurant is open six days a week and serves excellent local fare. It would be a shame not to attempt to taste everything, but a true crime to miss out on the *crocotini di asparagi* (asparagus croquettes) and duck-filled *plin* (a homemade pasta dish similar to ravioli). The modern wine cantina and hotel shop are found in the converted stone farmhouse behind the villa, which also houses the restaurant and two spectacular suites.

Villa Tiboldi is located in the tiny town of Roero, just over an hour from Turin and two hours from Milan. A stop on Butterfield & Robinson's bike tour through Piedmont, the hotel is certainly up and coming. For activities, the villa offers bikes for touring, wine tastings, carriage rides, and day trips to Canale's local market.

THE ROOMS

The main villa's four rooms are junior suites and are elegantly styled with soft pastel color schemes, painted ceilings, and silk drapes. Traditional four-poster beds with sheer curtains,

A vineyard tapestry

claw-foot tubs, and custom furnishings add a romantic touch, as do the French doors that open out to tiny balconies overlooking the property and rolling vine-covered hills below. Room 3 in the main villa is particularly fanciful, done in varying shades of green with an airy, light-blue bathroom (pictured above). Two large balcony windows allow streams of warm morning light to enter the room while a small mahogany writer's desk and antique mannequin give the room a whimsical feminine charm. Three rooms nestled into the small brick cottage by the pool offer uninterrupted vineyard views. The two large suites and double room in the converted stone barn are above the hotel's ground-floor restaurant and are the hotel's most eclectic rooms. According to Roberto, the largest corner suite

provides the best night's sleep on account of its cool stone interior and historic connection to the land. Both rooms feature bright red floral and bold striped fabrics and furnishings that are more contemporary than those in the main villa. The exposed ceiling beams, stone floors, and modern wooden bathrooms showcase the room's modest origins, while the vibrant colors, king-sized bed, and eclectic light fixtures add a more modern feel. The diversity in Villa Tiboldi's rooms is a tribute to the creative prowess of Patrizia. Each is decorated with care, and many of the rooms' objects are the triumphant results of Patrizia's many years of antique hunting. The decoration and variety of the accommodations at Villa Tiboldi exemplify the hotel's devotion to catering to all types of guests.

The custom details in the villa's guestrooms (left); a tub to remember in Room 3

The fresh look of Villa Tiboldi's main exterior

ABOVE *Room 3's luxurious bed* | OPPOSITE *The villa's pool surrounded by vineyards*

LA VILLA HOTEL

CASALOTTO/MOMBARUZZO, PIEMONTE

ITHIN five minutes of arriving at La Villa Hotel, a glass of Prosecco has been poured and offered from the bar, which incidentally doubles as the hotel's reception desk. So immediately congenial and casual is the welcome that when asked whether you'd like to be taken to your room you can't help but be somewhat taken aback. How is it that already you are so at ease and have yet to unpack? The comfortable atmosphere at La Villa is encouraged and exemplified by owners Nicola and Chris Norton. It's not uncommon to be greeted by Nicola from behind the bar in the morning in her bikini top, or catch Chris stealing an afternoon nap by the pool.

The Irish-English couple bought the villa four years ago, emigrating to Italy with their two young daughters and cat to make the small vineyard town of Casalotto in the Piedmont region their permanent home. A stately seventeenth-century palazzo painted pale pink with light-blue shutters, La Villa stands out among the surrounding green vineyards. An English-style garden with miniature hedgerows, narrow gravel paths, and bushes of lavender and rosemary fills the interior courtyard, and a smaller, well-tended rose garden can be found alongside the villa's entrance. The garden's abundant fragrant flowers and plants infuse the air with their sweet scent. The carefully pruned gardens and Chris and Nicola's darling daughters' British accents are more or less the only remaining emblems of their

Lush lavender delight at La Villa Hotel

Anglo heritage; everything else at La Villa Hotel is meant to ingratiate the guest into the Italian way of life—much like Nicola and Chris did when they first arrived.

A recently opened restaurant above the breakfast room provides Nicola the perfect podium to present her vast knowledge of local wines and demonstrate her talents in the kitchen. When occupancy is high and a number of guests have expressed an interest in staying in for dinner, Juliet Jarvis, the head chef, and Nicola will prepare a hearty four-course meal featuring flavorful local dishes paired with four different local wines. The result is an equally gluttonous and educational lesson in the bounty of the surrounding countryside. Juliet's meringue and strawberry dessert served in a wine goblet is worthy of special request.

Just an hour from Turin and Milan and only forty-five minutes from seaside Genova, La Villa is easily accessible from major airports. Two of Piedmont's culinary hot spots and wine production centers, Asti and Alba, are within a half hour's drive and make easy day trips for sightseeing and indulging in the local delicacies and world-renowned Barolo and Barbera wines. The profound pioneering spirit of Nicola and Chris has led them to become experts in the local culture. Nicola, a pronounced wine connoisseur, is happy to reserve visits at her favorite local vineyards and will sometimes accompany you to ensure you take home only the best. The hotel also offers painting and furniture restoration courses. Sunset at La Villa Hotel is its finest hour, and fortunately both Chris and Nicola are aware of that, quickly suggesting an accompanying glass of wine. The setting sun is best appreciated from the hotel's pool terrace or from the ridgeline path just a few minutes' stroll from the hotel. Both offer tantalizing views of the sun's glorious rays bathing the hills and streaming down between the countless rows of grapevines in the vineyards.

THE ROOMS

The thirteen rooms and suites at La Villa Hotel are pleasantly decorated with locally found furnishings and textiles along with varying design accents from Morocco, France, and rural Italy. Each room features simple cotton linens that put the focus on the room's furnishings and custom details. Due to the villa's careful refurbishment and natural elegance, little ornamentation is needed to make the place feel well-appointed. The iron railing on the balconies, original wood doors, vaulted ceilings, and antique tile floors afford the villa ample sophistication. Nicola and Chris spent a year and a half hunting through Piedmont collecting antiques and period furniture in hopes of highlighting the villa's rich history and enlightening their guests on local history. The occasional antiquated farming tool—like a nineteenth-century chestnut press or

an antique wine-corking machine—can be found mounted on the wall or in the corner of the honeymoon suite's entryway. The traditional objects and attention to local history give La Villa Hotel a warm sense of place and encourage the guest to learn more about the surrounding area.

Room 4, one of the three hotel rooms that make up the so-called French Quarter of the Villa, is particularly soothing, with its ivory colored furnishings, billowing curtains, and iron balcony overlooking the rose garden. A warm bubble bath in the magnificent curved claw-foot tub overlooking the vineyards is the ideal cure for jetlag. In contrast is room 7, whose large wooden armoire and headboard are a deep chestnut brown, accentuated by gold-and-tan-checked throw pillows and a dark brown duvet. The room is decidedly less feminine but no less elegant, with a large inviting bed and balcony onto the garden. The bathrooms at La Villa Hotel are all recently remodeled, and most have fabulous walk-in rain showers. The shower in room 7 is particularly spacious and inviting with a full window view of the rolling vineyards. The variety of the rooms' shape, design, and color scheme is considerable, so asking the owners for specific details when booking and voicing your preferences can make all the difference to your stay. Each room, however, shares the delightful and thoughtful touches of bedside tea-sets, homemade soap, floral arrangements from the garden, and cozy throw blankets perfect for an afternoon nap.

The Villa Hotel's
classic appeal

ABOVE *The perfect place to nap (top); the English garden in the courtyard (below)* | OPPOSITE *The cream-colored look of the Villa's French Quarter guestrooms*

JK CAPRI

JK Capri is movie-set cool: immaculately styled and perfectly fashionable. Being whisked from the ferry port in the JK Capri white golf cart is just the beginning of a thoughtful and design-centric approach to hotel service. The hotel is laid out just like a private home, albeit one whose interiors are superbly designed and well appointed. The entryway is the first glimpse into owner Ori Kafri's new level of hotel interior design. A round mahogany table, teeming with orchids and coffee-table books on style icons, artists, and various pop-culture subjects, is the centerpiece of the black-and-white-checkered marble-floored foyer. The reception area is a mere sitting room off the foyer, with an antique desk and two chairs. Through the foyer is the open space of the living room, which is buffered by a contemporary library and elegant dining room. Each room is brighter, more intricately designed, and more striking than the last. The library contains a vibrant array of floor-to-ceiling bookshelves, a white couch with hot-colored pillows, a kitschy blue-and-white backgammon board, and the requisite flat-screen television with extensive DVD collection. The dining room is used for dinner upon request but otherwise maintains an informal elegance with silver painted chairs and custom chrome light fixtures. There is also a stylish glass pitcher of iced tea on the dining room hutch, further establishing the informal but chic tone. The living room,

The Midas touch of JK Capri

library, and dining room all have French doors that open onto the hotel's spacious front porch. The teak deck and furniture with plush white cushions is an exclusive party venue waiting to happen. JK Capri matchbooks done in the hotel's signature light-blue-and-white-striped motif adorn each table, adding a colorful element.

However, the best advocate of the hotel's attitude is its owner, Ori Kafri. With an enviable mixture of ease and purpose, Kafri is clearly the source behind his hotel's eye-catching and posh décor. In his linen and loafers outfit, Kafri is emblematic of contemporary Italian hospitality—eager to discuss his recent magazine venture and future hotel projects. His passion is palpable, and his knowledge of the industry is extensive. He is a positive force in a country that oftentimes rests on its laurels. With two boutique hotels, JK Place in Florence and JK Capri, plus an operational share in the new *Firenze* magazine, Kafri is an innovator in his homeland's hotel industry—and his properties are a testament to that.

JK Capri has every five-star luxury, plus a stunning location overlooking Capri's *marina grande* and the cerulean sea. There is a decent-sized gym, which seems larger owing to its savvy use of multiple mirrored walls. The spa, done by renowned ESPA, has a menu of tempting treatments and services, including one in which after being painted with a local mineral spread you are left to float in a shallow bathtub for maximum

relaxation. The pool is a scenic affair, with chaise longues on two sides, and attentive drink and snack service. Lunch is served on the side deck of the hotel, just off the polished bar, and fittingly serves up a most delicious caprese salad.

The island of Capri is a popular tourist destination, and its main marina is constantly abuzz, making JK Capri's convenient location even more appealing. A short walk down the hill puts you right in the thick of things, while a taxi is easily summoned to take you up to Anacapri, the hill town of Capri, for lunch or to Capri's own natural wonder, the Blue Grotto. The hotel's concierge will also arrange boat tours around the island, private boat and helicopter transfers, and guided walking tours of the island. True indulgence, though, is to be found by lazing an afternoon away at JK Capri, flitting between the pool, deck lounge, and tantalizing book collection.

THE ROOMS

The twenty-two rooms and suites are done in a classic nautical motif. A clean and fresh feel is revealed through a navy-and-white color scheme, a simple chrome corner chair, black-and-white prints of yachts, and a set of white painted wooden chairs and coffee table. The Lucite desk and ample flat-screen television plus all-tile bathroom with walk-in shower reflect the multiple-star quality of the hotel, while the view of the sea and mainland in the distance reminds you of the hotel's singular location. The "master bedroom with sea view" has dome-shaped French doors that lead out to a small terrace over the harbor and attractive closets with sisal carpet–lined floors, showing yet again the thoughtful detail employed in the décor at JK Capri.

ABOVE *The omnipresent initials also on the bed (left); the punch of pink in the living room (right)*

OPPOSITE *The immaculate and stunning dining room*

CLOCKWISE FROM TOP LEFT
*Plush white chairs and sofas on
the teak deck; the clean look of
JK Capri's guestrooms*

OPPOSITE *The custom
style of the bar*

OVERLEAF *The canopy bed of
a deluxe room and the mesmerizing view of Capri's waterfront*

VILLA CIMBRONE

genuine hideaway, the Amalfi coast's Villa Cimbrone is accessible only on foot. The secret-gardenlike entrance is reached by following charming blue-and-white majolica tile signs that begin in Ravello's town square and lead you a quarter mile down a winding but beautiful stone pathway. The rustic path is, in fact, the perfect induction into the hotel's beautiful authentic style.

Ravello is a pedestrian town tucked into the hillside 650 feet above sea level just above Amalfi. In order to enter, you must leave your car at one of the two town parking lots before climbing a few stairs to the main square. The hotel arranges for you to be met by their porter in a golf cart next to the parking lot. He will then take your luggage and direct you to the town square and the beginning of your journey. Easy enough, but bear in mind that it's best to hand as much of your luggage as possible over to the porter, given the path's length and sometimes steep declines.

The villa's stone facade is covered completely in ivy, and the front garden boasts an amazing palm tree, thick and bountiful and particularly gorgeous at night when it is lit by floodlights and casts its tremendous shadow on the ground. The massive ancient wooden doors lock after 8 P.M. when the villa's public gardens close to the public. Guests must then ring the bell and give their name to be let in personally, like an access code to an exclusive club. Originally the

property of the king of Sicily and Naples, Ladislao D'Angio Durazzo, the villa's regal roots are evident upon entry. A vine-covered pergola frames a view down toward the cliff's edge and out to the sea, while the castlelike villa stands tall over the immense lawn and manicured gardens that surround the property. In 1403, the king gave the property to the Fusco family, who owned it until 1864, when it was then appropriated for the Amici family of Atrani. Then in 1904 an Englishman and member of Parliament, Ernest William Beckett, who later became known as Lord Grimthorpe, bought the villa and turned the gardens into what they are today. After Beckett's death, in the 1950s, Villa Cimbrone was sold to the Vuilleumiers, a local family, who opened the gardens to the public and turned the villa into an exclusive hotel with a fine-dining restaurant.

Villa Cimbrone has one of the most stunning settings you will ever behold. The colors of the fifteen-acre garden, redesigned in the nineteenth century and boasting hundreds of varieties of flowers and plants, beckon visitors from all over the world. Unbelievably fragrant and lush, the park is embellished with works of art, including temples, gazebos, and marble and bronze statues, guaranteeing a serene yet dazzling stroll. It's no wonder the Villa Cimbrone is one of the top wedding destinations in Italy. The famous "Terrace of Infinity," an image of which domi-

English gardens at Villa Cimbrone

nates Ravello's postcards, is found at the end of the villa's gardens, and its row of classic marble busts and panoramic view are nothing short of inspirational. The best part is that as a guest of the hotel it's all yours in the evenings, making cocktail hour a unique and sensuous treat.

The villa has a rather large peanut-shaped pool with stylish lounge chairs and is currently adding a spa. There is an elegant restaurant that serves nouveau Italian cuisine, in which each dish offers a more surprising take on the traditional presentation than the last. The chocolate dessert is a threefold offering of chocolate served in liquid, cake, and gelatin form. The rooftop terrace is the site for the complimentary breakfast. The panoramic southern view of the Amalfi coast is an ideal way to start your day. The rest of the day can be spent touring Ravello's historic villas and gardens, other famous hotels (the infinity pool at Hotel Caruso is a must-see), and quaint shops. The jewelry store next to the church in the main piazza has exquisite handmade coral necklaces and earrings, which apparently tempted visitor Hillary Clinton, whose photograph adorns the front window. In July, there is a world-renowned music festival, featuring operas and concerts by some of the world's best musicians. Often, the musicians fly into Ravello on helicopters, landing at the Villa Cimbrone, which boasts the town's only helipad. Witnessing a landing is yet another reminder of the villa's enduring royal feel.

THE ROOMS

There are nineteen rooms in the villa as well as two suites and four junior suites. The layout of the villa has for the most part remained unchanged since it was a private home. The result for guests is an intimate experience. The library and the adjacent terrace are decorated with antique furnishings and original books and artifacts belonging to the previous owner. The emerald green tile floors demonstrate the understated elegance of the villa's décor. The villa was recently remodeled under the supervision of Italy's superintendent of works of art, so the many frescoes, antique furnishings, marble and majolica floors, and original works of art and rare books all appear as Lord Grimthorpe left them.

The bedrooms are named after flowers that grow in the garden. The interiors are done in the local coastal Italian style with majolica tile floors in blues, greens, and pinks, while the walls are done in a relief stucco decoration that gives them a stately feel. The color schemes of the rooms reflect the palette of the landscape outside, and the furnishings are modest and comfortable enough for you to forget them and focus on the true highlight: the view. The Fresco suite is enormous, with two floor-length windows looking straight out to sea. It has a quaint sitting porch and a sizable marble bathroom, but it's the room's dimensions and painted tiled floor that are the suite's showstopping elements.

The eye-catching brilliance of the Fresco Suite

CLOCKWISE FROM TOP LEFT
*The view from the Terrace of
Infinity; the ancient Roman
style windows of the villa;
the garden's vaulted gazebo*

OPPOSITE *The entrance
to the Terrace of Infinity*

CASA ANGELINA

ESPITE an entrance right off the main drag, Casa Angelina's gate and white sign are easily overlooked, mostly because the main road along Italy's famed Amalfi coast does everything but drag. Whether it's due to the mesmerizing postcard-worthy panoramas, the dramatic cliffs to the side of the road, or the white-knuckle narrow encounters with oncoming traffic, distracted drivers are ensured—but so too is Casa Angelina's hideaway status.

Located in Praiano, an up-and-coming destination on the coast between Amalfi and Positano, Casa Angelina stands out with its all-white contemporary design that dramatically contrasts with the rich blues and greens of the surrounding land and water. Originally built in 1975 and remodeled in 2004, Casa Angelina is raising eyebrows along the Amalfi coast with its distinct departure from the norm. The purposeful all-white interiors, which include white maple stairs, a Philippe Stark light system, and all-white bathroom design, plus handmade ceramic furniture and paved rooms by Vietri all in white, demonstrate the hotel's novel dedication to a clean, simple interior. Further innovation is evidenced through Casa Angelina's panoramic elevator—the only one of its kind in Italy. The elevator is wall-to-wall glass, giving off a sense of delicious weightlessness for the passenger as his or her gaze stretches out along the Gulf of Salerno, catching the hazy outline of Capri in the distance. The elevator travels all the way down

through a cave to the rocky private beach, which, along with the terrace pool, provides ample excuse for lounging around. Casa Angelina is also savvy to the hotel industry's current trend of branding and has developed its own signature fragrance, which is pumped through the hotel's ventilation system and available for sale at the front desk.

Undeniably social in design, Casa Angelina has a scenic bar with a colorful Cuban-inspired mural, which provides the hotel's largest departure from the all-white interior, plus large picture windows out to the sea-view terrace and pool. The lobby lounge is a row of white couches and tables, perfect for snuggling up with a magazine or as one couple did, checking their email from their laptop. Lunch service is available by the pool and on the terrace and offers a menu with a variety of fresh entrée salads and typical seaside fare. The view is the ideal backdrop to a pleasant and carefree meal. The atmosphere during the day and early evening is loungelike, with guests milling about in an array of sarong-style wear, reading material in hand. Cocktail hour is at the same lobby bar, and the couches that earlier held sun-drenched nappers now cater to well-dressed young couples showing off their newly acquired suntans. For those so inclined, there's also a Cigar Room below the bar. The gym buff will also be pleased to find a modern, well-equipped exercise room complete with indoor pool, Pilates classes, and custom massage services. Upon

The night lights of Positano from Casa Angelina's pool deck

THE ROOMS

The white-on-white décor is even more pronounced in Casa Angelina's guest rooms. The forty rooms including one spectacular suite and one incredible junior bear no trace of color other than that provided by the welcome fruit basket, achieving the desired effect of tranquility. Once your eye adjusts to the bright white, it travels outward, through the tall glass windows and doors to the porch, seeking the rich color of the immense sea-blurred horizon. Both suites are located on the top floor, offering the most breathtaking view across the Bay of Salerno, with Capri in the distance and Positano nestled within those wondrous drop-off coastal mountains. Well suited to honeymooners and romantic liaisons, the two top-floor suites have large terraces allowing for all-day sunbathing, evening cocktails, and late-night stargazing in complete privacy.

In fact, all forty rooms have private balconies so the guest can feel intimate with the hotel's seafront location. The rooms are all outfitted with today's requisite plasma televisions, Internet connections, down comforters, and personal temperature controls. When choosing your room it is wise to ask for rooms at the ends of each floor (the 100 or the 112 numbers) so that the balcony has one side completely open to the view and offers more privacy from other guests. The bathroom in deluxe room 200 is delightful, with a discreet but alluring sea view direct from the tub and shower. Bath products from L'Occitane and an ingenious bathmat with a plush terry top and thick rubber bottom provide a luxurious feel and remind you that it's the little things that often matter most when away from home. Although the rooms are devoid of rich colors and lush fabrics, Casa Angelina proves that a romantic ambience can be created in starkness just as easily as in softness.

request, the hotel also arranges shopping and day trips to destinations like Pompeii, Capri, and Sorrento. The staff at Casa Angelina, particularly Gaetano Bellipanni, is quick to greet the guest with a smile and warm suggestion of what to order when the carefree indecision that comes with being truly relaxed hits.

The most decadent pleasure, however, is the penthouse restaurant, Un Piano nel Cielo, which offers both indoor and outdoor seating areas, used for both a plentiful breakfast and a more formal dinner. The restaurant experience begins with a smiling greeting from the host as soon as one steps off the elevator and is highlighted by an average of three attendants per table. Truly spoiled is the couple who, while dining outside, can clink their Prosecco-filled glasses over the chef's flavorful *amuse-bouche* and marvel at the divine view of the lights of Positano. The menu is filled with innovative treatments of local seafood dishes and traditional pastas providing a truly gourmet experience. Locally made almond milk is available upon request and makes for a sweet bedtime tonic.

ABOVE *The modern fixtures in the bathroom of the suite*

OPPOSITE *Perfect symmetry in the lobby*

ABOVE *The Master suite* | OPPOSITE *The picture windows of the hotel bar (top) and the never tiring view of the Gulf of Salerno (bottom)*

MEZZATORRE

ISCHIA, CAMPANIA

Tucked away on a peninsula in Forio, the tony part of the mountainous island of Ischia, in the Bay of Naples, Mezzatorre Resort & Spa commands an unparalleled seaside position. A member of the Leading Hotels of the World, the hotel is named for the surviving half of a brick-red sixteenth-century tower that rises up from the rocky peninsula and offers 180-degree views of the sea from the suites and side porches. The sweeping view of the ocean and mainland far off in the distance provides the height of relaxation. In fact, the very tip of the peninsula just in front of the tower is equipped with a small stone bench and is aptly named "the point of contemplation."

Between the vibrant island flowers and the twinkling cerulean sea, the scenery at Mezzatorre is spellbindingly gorgeous. Built into the side of a hill, the hotel's layout is separated into tiers, providing an array of mesmerizing vantage points. Starting from the bottom and traveling upward, the hotel offers a small protected swimming lagoon, a salt water pool and a thatched-roof restaurant, a row of white lounge chairs and couches, an indoor gym and spa located in the tower's ground floor, and, at the top, an elegant restaurant with a rooftop lounge area and large stone veranda overlooking the sea. Choosing the day's best seating area could be Mezzatorre's sole challenge—well, that and deciding what time to schedule your facial or what to order for lunch.

The alluring landscape and marvelous architecture of Mezzatorre

Served in the poolside restaurant whose linen curtains are attractively held together with custom coral-shaped rope ties, lunch includes a bountiful seafood and traditional antipasti spread, where seconds (and thirds!) are inevitable. The baskets of delicious homemade *crocattini*—crunchy bread knots made with spicy pepper and almonds—are quickly refilled by attentive waiters.

Ischia is known for its abundance of spas, and Mezzatorre's White Spa is among the best in the country. Its signature bath products, particularly the shampoo and conditioner—another rarity in Italian hotels—are worth hoarding. Located below the grand suite in the tower and occupying the lowest point of the peninsula, the spa provides a host of beauty and wellness services, but it is the outdoor wide-bed massage tables that are most notable. Mezzatorre also has a small indoor gym, which is clean and comfortable. Given its popularity among honeymooners and couples, Mezzatorre caters to the romance of the setting by offering a cocktail hour with hors d'oeuvres in its outdoor piano bar. The beautiful terrace restaurant provides the ultimate in romantic dining, with its cliff-top view out to the sea and small, intimate tables. Given Mezzatorre's tranquil and pleasing nature, choosing anything but the most decadent option feels incongruous. Instead embrace the impulse to indulge and spend your days lounging and relaxing—that's what vacations are for.

THE ROOMS

Although the tower is the namesake of the hotel, it houses less than a third of the hotel's fifty-nine guest rooms. Despite the large number of rooms, Mezzatorre maintains an intimate feel through its secluded peninsula location. The majority of the guest rooms are tucked back into the hillside and offer private gardens and terraces. The views vary and improve the closer they are to the sea. The garden and terrace rooms are more private, though the tower rooms, albeit smaller and tighter, give the hotel its signature appeal. The tower rooms are preferable simply for their all-encompassing views of the property and the sea. Decorated in a pink-and-peach color scheme, the rooms are cozy, with comfortable full mattresses and goose down pillows. The marble bathroom's considerable shower pressure and remarkable bath products from Mezzatorre's White Spa ensure a more than pleasing bathing experience. Moreover, the tower itself feels like a private enclave for those staying there. The front sitting room is well appointed with custom light fixtures, antique marble tables, and deep couches. Three side porches, one on each level, offer great views of the sea and the property plus comfortable chaise longues to take it all in.

The tower's Grand Suite is brand new and perhaps the most palatial suite in this book. Occupying an entire floor, the suite is comprised of a sitting room, an en-suite bathroom whose bathtub is situated in front of a large bay window showcasing the boat-laden cove on the right side of the peninsula, and a large bedroom with canopied bed. The room's best attributes, though, are its outdoor spaces. A wide hallway leads you out from the bedroom onto an expansive deck with a Jacuzzi, two chaise longues facing the sea and the peninsula's "thinking point," a table and chairs from which to enjoy an intimate meal, plus a cushioned sitting area. The room is a sumptuous fantasy come true, with all the trimmings of grand-style living, including a white-canopied king bed, flat-screen television, Internet hook-up, iPod dock, a separate dressing area with dressing table, and a massive private terrace. The terrace is the ideal backdrop for a private, romantic encounter. The view, though the same from the shared porches, seems infinitely more personal from the suite's grand terrace.

ABOVE AND OPPOSITE
*Sweeping romance
and decadent views
at Mezzatorre*

OVERLEAF *The arched view
from a tower suite (left);*
CLOCKWISE FROM TOP LEFT
*The mesmerizing boat
traffic; the striking interior
from the tower's lobby; the
sail cloth ceiling from al fresco
dining; coral rope detail in
the pool restaurant*

CA MARIA ADELE

VENEZIA, VENETO

RARELY does a hotel stay leave you so content that you'd be willing to pay more the next time. Even more surprising is the fact that the hotel is located in one of Italy's more expensive cities, Venice, where a simple panino can run you eight euros. Ca Maria Adele, a small boutique hotel in Venice's quiet Dorsoduro neighborhood, encourages that very reaction. The hotel is housed in a sixteenth-century palace just steps from the glorious white-domed church Santa Maria della Salute.

Charming but not cute, sophisticated but comfortable, Ca Maria Adele appeals as much to the aesthetic as to the weary vacationer. With its attention to detail and impeccable service, the hotel distinguishes itself as a haven from the chaos of Venice, engaging all the senses. The intimate front sitting room stimulates the eye with contrasting design elements and colors. A small black marble fireplace blooms with hot-pink coral, and the mantle is adorned with sea urchins and starfish-treasures from the owners' recent trip to Capri—while Moroccan sconces feature painted black hands holding small, jeweled lamps. The nose tingles from the incense reed arrangements in tall glass bottles in every guest room. Judy Garland ballads play faintly in the sitting room, lobby, and Moroccan-style sun porch, setting the hotel's tone. Upon their return to the hotel in the afternoon, guests are surprised and spoiled with late-afternoon trays of lemon gelato, crescent almond cookies, and strawberries delivered fresh to their rooms. How the proprietors have the trays waiting for each guest at exactly the right time remains a mystery. Last is the luxurious turndown treat of rose petals, moisturizing facial spray, and a roomy terry robe, urging guests to feel cozy. Where else can such a state of relaxation be so effortlessly achieved? And what better antidote to the maddening crowds of Venice than a hotel whose main goal is to comfort you on all fronts?

Set away from the hustle and bustle of Piazza San Marco on the decidedly more tame side of the Grand Canal, Ca Maria Adele faces the beautiful church of Santa Maria della Salute and is a short walk to the Peggy Gugghenehim Collection and the Accademia bridge. The Santa Maria della Salute ferry stop is a two-minute walk from the entrance of the hotel, and on the local number 1 ferry boat Piazza San Marco is just one stop away. For those who just cannot fathom Venice without a gondola ride, the hotel appeases with a private water entrance and a picturesque wooden dock romantically adorned with white petunias and lanterns.

Dusk is when Ca Maria Adele's location is most alluring. The city seems to quiet down in the evenings, and the sunset view becomes precious. Ca Maria Adele is near two great viewing spots: the steps of Santa Maria della Salute looking over to Venice's city center and Dorsoduro's long

The covered serenity of Ca Maria Adele's secluded location

waterside quay looking over to the opposite island of Giudecca all aglow in the pink light. A quiet special dinner can be found at Linea dall'Ombra, just down an alleyway from the hotel, so close that getting lost is virtually impossible—which, after a day touring Venice, is particularly appealing. Furthermore, the ever-attentive owners, Nicolo and Alessio Campa, and their staff are always quick with suggestions and eager to ease and enhance your visit however possible. For the guest who feels his or her needs are often not met, then Ca Maria Adele should provide them with their next destination.

THE ROOMS

Room 321 or, the Sala Noir, as it is known, is one of Ca Maria Adele's four "concept rooms." Sala Noir is the favorite of owner Alessio Campa, who will readily share the room's specific origin and design concept. The room is dominated by a massive black glass chandelier that emerges serpentine-like from the yellow silk pleated ceiling. The walls are a rich chocolate-colored Fortuny fabric, while the two wing chairs are done in yellow-gold velvet and the duvet in a shimmering maroon. The effect is decidedly masculine, though its pronounced ambience will appeal to both sexes, and couples will revel in the sensual

feel of the scalloped sheer gold curtains and potted palms. The room is a duplex, with the bathroom upstairs done entirely in wall-to-wall black subway tile, illuminated by a fluorescent square mirror; the tile is used most effectively in the enormous walk-in rain shower, whose shower head is the size of a doormat. An impressive array of toiletries will appease the female guest, though it is men who will best appreciate the dark and iridescent color scheme of the bathroom.

The hotel's ten deluxe rooms feature a less striking design, instead using the same soothing and fresh beige-and-cream Fortuny fabric found in the breakfast room. The neutral color scheme mixed with mahogany furnishings, antique desks, and soft carpeting make the rooms feel like comfortable sanctuaries, ideal after a day of touring in Venice. Suite 336 is a particularly appealing room, located on the top floor of the hotel with small picture windows framing views of Santa Maria della Salute, the water between Dorsoduro and Giudecca, and the quaint street. The multiple windows also allow for pleasant seaside cross breezes. The bed is a raised platform bed with a large free-standing Jacuzzi tub placed at its foot. The most ingenious touch, though, is the flat-screen television attached to the wooden ceiling beams that cross above the bed.

OPPOSITE *The strong Moroccan influence of the terrace*

OVERLEAF *The neutral palette of the breakfast room (left);* CLOCKWISE FROM TOP LEFT *The black-tile bathroom of Sala Noir; the well adorned lobby sitting room; the owner's black Murano glass chandelier; the ruffled detail of Sala Noir*

PALAZZO BAUER

Hardly a hideaway, with its red-canopied and gold-embossed facade trumpeting its elegance down the Grand Canal, the Palazzo Bauer—an authentic eighteenth-century palazzo with an unbeatable location minutes away from Piazza San Marco and Harry's Bar and footsteps from the city's best shopping—is one of Venice's most luxurious hotels. Given that the palazzo has eighty-two rooms and thirty-eight suites, and its neighboring sister hotel, the Bauer Hotel, has ninety-one rooms and eighteen suites, it can hardly be called a discovery. Yet if approached with the foreknowledge of a certain room and the hotel's exclusive terrace restaurant, Settimo Cielo, the Palazzo Bauer can transform itself into the most intimate of hideaways conveniently located only minutes from the action.

The Palazzo Bauer and Hotel Bauer properties were given a fifty-million-dollar facelift in 1997 by Fracesca Bortolotto Possati, the granddaughter of Arnaldo Bennati and heir to the family's properties. Possatti personally oversaw the extensive renovations and was behind the decision to divide the two properties in order to attract two separate markets and making the Palazzo Bauer the first-class option of the two.

Entering or exiting the palazzo through the water entrance provides the quintessential Venetian experience. The popular waterfront terrace that is shared with the Hotel Bauer runs right alongside the small dock and allows for the perfect amount of audience for your cinematic departure or arrival by water taxi. It also proves a charming spot to appreciate the marvel that is Venice while sipping a coffee or glass of Prosecco. The front door of the palazzo presents its subtle refinement in the form of attractive porters dressed in red and black who usher you into the small lobby decorated in gilt mirrors, an Asian wooden desk, and a delectable old-fashioned key box displaying the ornate silver-plated and tasseled guest keys.

The palazzo's best-kept secret is its seventh-floor dining terrace and lounge. Open for breakfast only and closing at 11 A.M., the Settimo Cielo ("seventh sky") offers a panoramic vista of Venice unlike any other. The pity is that it isn't open for cocktails, given the sheer romance of the view. Instead guests can witness the morning sunlight glint off the canal and buildings below, and from the terrace's specific vantage point the historic and current-day shipping lanes of Venice are crystal clear. You can almost imagine the clipper ships that must have once dominated the seascape as they came to Venice to trade or return home from exploration.

The amenities at the Palazzo Bauer cover all the bases for the luxury standards of today's guests. There is a two-room spa, with a talented masseuse, an outdoor Jacuzzi with skyline views that can be reserved for private sessions, a small

The antique key box at Palazzo Bauer's front desk

ABOVE *View down the Grand Canal from Room 306 (left) and the plush lobby sitting room (right)*

OPPOSITE *The doge red awnings of the Palazzo Bauer*

OVERLEAF *Room 306, aptly known as The Jewel Box*

FOLLOWING SPREAD *The view at sunset from Settimo Cielo*

but well-equipped gym, and wireless connection available, at a premium, in the rooms. For diversion, the city of Venice awaits, and its many treasures are within arm's reach of the hotel.

THE ROOMS

Room 306, dubbed, affectionately and appropriately, the Jewel Box, is tucked into a corner of the third floor with arched windows on two walls. The room is swathed floor to ceiling in a Valentine-red fabric originally designed for the Bennati family by the famous Venetian fabric house Rubelli. A reliance on one motif runs the risk of overwhelming, but the room's architecture, craftsmanship, and delicate antique furnishings turn the monochromatic design into a soothing haven. Unabashedly Venetian in its opulence, the room's tight dimensions and dual water views give it a boatlike feel. The front window faces out to the island of Giudecca over the white dome of Santa Maria della Salute, while the corner window offers a direct view down the

Grand Canal toward Rialto. Waking up in room 306 with both windows thrown open to dramatic effect is a singular experience. The room not only feels nautical, with its canal views, but also captures the movement of the lagoon beneath it. Such a prominent view and lush surroundings make guests feel truly immersed in Venice and all its glory. Order the complimentary morning cappuccino, close the fabric-covered pocket doors, and climb back into bed to take in the distinct sights, sounds, and even smells of one of the most incredible cities in the world. A popular room, even among celebrities, it is wise to call well ahead of time to reserve room 306 or one of the other few canal-facing rooms. Although the palazzo has many beautiful rooms, they are all quite different and the guest's experience can be greatly affected by the room selection. If a view is paramount, or perhaps the size of the bathroom, then it is best you specify these needs and desires prior to booking. Being satisfied at the palazzo is an exceptional experience and one well worth planning.

PALAZZO MOCENIGO

An inspirational haven for the nineteenth-century poet Lord Byron and perennial host to famous politicians, artists, and noblemen such as the prince of Savoy, Palazzo Mocenigo continues to exude the same glamour and intrigue it did when owned by the Mocenigo family over five hundred years ago. A masterful sixteenth-century palace on the Grand Canal, Palazzo Mocenigo is now the precious center jewel in the crown of Venice's lauded Bauer Hotel group, owned by Venetian Francesca Bortolotto Possati. The palace commands an enviable position on the Grand Canal between the Rialto bridge and Piazza San Marco. And with an elegant facade featuring an iron-gated water entrance, private boat dock, and regal blue awnings over each window, its centuries-old allure remains intact.

A grand canal palace fit for a doge, Palazzo Mocenigo offers seven separate bedrooms and is more than aptly suited for large events, holding up to 140 people. Yet the grandness of the place, split into three separate rentals or offered as one whole, never dulls its inherent sense of intimacy and its distinctive personality. The palace presents two gloriously Venetian entrances: a breathtakingly gothic water entrance complete with dangling lanterns and striped dock poles, and a second, secret-garden-like entrance from the street. The courtyard off the street entrance presents a full Italian-style

The noble entrance hall

garden with magnolia trees that is one of the few remaining Venetian gardens intact from the sixteenth century.

However enchanting the exterior may be, nothing quite prepares you for the opulence of the palace interiors. Beginning with the original stone-laid entryway with large chandeliers and an ancient stone staircase flanked by two torch-bearing marble statues, entering the palace is simply otherworldly. The main floor, the *piano nobile*, is overwhelming with its enormous dimensions of eighteen-foot ceilings and opposing walls of windows, one side overlooking the glorious Grand Canal and the other the charming Italian garden. The main entryway, immense at almost three thousand square feet, spans the entire length of the palace and is furnished with round center tables, a white grand piano, and four long couches, which all look like dollhouse furniture, dwarfed by the room's palatial size. The custom-made floor is nothing short of spectacular. Inlaid Venetian mosaic marble sparkles in the sunlight, reminiscent of a time when beauty and craftsmanship were found in the details. The adjacent salons share the same exquisite floor details and are filled with only the finest of antiques, Murano glass chandeliers and sconces, and a large damask tapestry. The living room has a gorgeous marble fireplace with Bassano ceramic tiles, while the sofas are covered in Rubelli's fabric using the owner's original family

print. The perfunctory kitchen (staffed by Bauer Hotel on request) and library, along with the *piano nobile*'s other four bedrooms, are back on the garden end of the palace. Only one bedroom on the *piano nobile* claims the regal honor of overlooking the Grand Canal, and with three balconies it is certainly fit for a queen.

THE ROOMS

The master suite on the *piano nobile* looks out directly over the Grand Canal and is swathed entirely in a robin's-egg-blue Rubelli's fabric—the bed, headboard, and walls all blend into one another's sumptuous luxury. The room is furnished with an antique desk, a large armoire, and an ornately beautiful washbasin designed in the form of a swan and decorated with precious gold leafing. The master suite also features a large dressing room with mirrored cabinets, a pink-and-gold bathroom with both tub and shower, and a gorgeous Murano glass chandelier. The ceiling is decoratively painted, and the floor has a similar intricate mosaic design. The opulence and grandeur of the room is undeniable, but it is softened by the warmth of the Rubelli's fabric.

The palace also has a one-bedroom apartment located on the first floor, called the *mezzanino*, or mezzanine, which features similar silk tapestries, mosaic floors, and antique furnishings. Albeit a bit darker and shorter than the floor upstairs, its view of the Grand Canal is equally memorable. The *mezzanino* is ideal for a couple hoping to spend an unforgettable and romantic night in a Venetian palace. There is also a cottage just behind the palace nestled in the garden with one and a half bedrooms known as Mocenigo Cottage. The duplex-style accommodation has a modern kitchen and small sofa bed, making it perfect for a couple with children looking to spend time living the Venetian lifestyle, right alongside a historic palace. Special requests for chef, babysitting, or butler service are available through the Hotel Bauer. Each part of the palace has daily housekeeping and is served by the hotel's resident caretaker. Despite the palace's ancient structure and rich sixteenth-century feel, the entire property features complimentary wireless connection. Whether a guest visits the palace for a grand event, a decadent family gathering, or for a once-in-a-lifetime overnight stay, its quixotic appearance and sensibility are indelible.

ABOVE *Murano glass dominates the living room (left); an antique wash basin in the master suite (right)*

OPPOSITE *The opulent master suite*

CLOCKWISE FROM TOP LEFT
*The water entrance; the
adorned central staircase;
the street entrance boasting
one of the few large
gardens in Venice*

OPPOSITE *The palazzo's
impressive Grand Canal
address*

CARDUCCI 76

CATTOLICA is a busy summer beach town on the Adriatic, twenty minutes south of Rimini. Though smaller and less cosmopolitan than Rimini, Cattolica provides a vivid glimpse into Italian beach culture. The town's main street runs parallel to the sea and is an overflowing thoroughfare, with hotels upon hotels on each side. The street is a director's dream, with large families sitting together on the hotel porches, wet children screaming and running to and from the beach, and gregarious promoters advertising their wares from concession stands. A glistening all-white 1920s beach villa, Carducci 76 sits tucked in between two gargantuan beachfront hotels on Cattolica's main drag. Named after its address, the boutique hotel's white facade and two-story structure is a clear departure from the other properties that dominate Cattolica's coastline. As soon as the wooden white gate of Carducci 76 slides open revealing a private underground garage, the property's purpose to provide a haven for its guests is gloriously clear.

The only fashion hotel in Cattolica, Carducci 76 is as innovative as it is singular. The hotel's décor draws from the natural elements water, fire, and air, and employs design motifs from the Far East. The contemporary design and luxe style of the thirty-eight-room hotel were conceived by its owner, Massimo Feretti, brother of Italian clothing designer Alberta Feretti, and his architect friend, Luca Sgroi. The hotel's two main Art Deco structures consist of the original beachfront villa and an identical front building, designed to reflect the original villa and separate it from the street. This front building houses the reception area, spa, and a few second-floor guest rooms. The lawn between the two buildings has been transformed into an Asian-inspired garden with a waterfall, a slim, horizontal reflecting pool, and large gray stones. According to the ever-courteous manager, Marco Bordoni, the garden is the nicest part of the hotel because of its peacefulness, symmetry, and exotic charm.

The exotic is in fact, just what Carducci 76 hopes most to offer. A marked departure from the style of its neighbors and the look of its casual host town, the lobby is a square room with antiqued mirrored reception desks, black cubes for seating, and light boxes with twigs in a row along the right wall. Continuing through the garden and into the lounge area of the original villa, the sophisticated style and contemporary feel become even more determined. Deep-set couches and modern wingback chairs are done in a stark palette of whites, grays, and blacks, and large black-and-white prints of nudes and eclectic African art hang on the walls. The natural element is again represented by the copious plant life in the room and the large bay windows looking out to the sea and the garden. Dried vines fan the ceiling of the arched hallway to the hotel's chic and popular restaurant, Vicolo Santa Lucia, while

Contemporary chic in the lounge of Carducci 76

potted orchids and large vases of birchwood adorn the various dark wooden and black console tables. Remarkably, the sleekness of the two-tone lounge area avoids feeling too posh for the beachcomber and instead lends itself well to nursing a sunburn or quenching a thirst. Custom details like thin rope trim running along the bottom wall moldings and dark, distressed wood floors maintain a beachside feel. The lounge's terrace is open for breakfast and lunch and has a great view out over the rainbow of umbrellas lining the beach. Umbrellas are a notable fixture of Italian beaches and do far more than just shield the sun. Grouped together by color and then lined up alongside one another like colored dominos along the beach, the umbrellas are actually markers of the separate beach clubs. A new color represents a new beach club and a new owner to whom you pay your rental fee. The aqua and royal blue umbrellas just in front of Carducci 76—the prettiest umbrellas on the beach—are available to guests free of charge. The hotel's pool, encased on three sides by high white wall dividers, is a pleasant alternative to the crowded beach and a respite from the hot Italian sun. A poolside cabana offers a shaded, chic area for drinks or a light lunch. The pool's infinity edge, unlike most, actually faces toward the villa, allowing the cascading water to present an intimate waterfall view for the restaurant patrons in the ground-floor restaurant.

With the beach as its focal point, Cattolica offers a host of beach-themed activities. Sailboat, windsurfer, and dune buggy rentals are available right outside the hotel doors, while the area's many shops, restaurants, and nightclubs keep the socially minded visitor easily entertained. Due to its family-oriented atmosphere, Cattolica has some wonderful casual restaurants, particularly Picadilly Mare, run by two engaging brothers. The hotel also offers a small workout room with a treadmill, weights, and sea view. The stated intent of Carducci 76 is to seduce its clients. Everything from the velvet-soft material of the bedcovers to the spa is meant to intensify the effects of the already soothing seaside location. Because the summer months tend to draw crowds to Cattolica, Carducci 76's masseuse and beautician recommends visiting during the cooler fall and winter months. That, she says, is when the restorative powers of the sea air and the tranquil beach are most effective at reducing stress.

THE ROOMS

The hotel has thirty-eight rooms including three signature suites. The Thai suite (pictured right) is located in one of the original villa's two turrets and has an actual tanning bed in the room for die-hard sun worshipers. The room's bed is alone in the octagonal turret and enjoys sparkling sea views from the three large bay windows. The suite has two large flat-screen televisions and a step-down bathroom with double vanities and a rain shower, ensuring a luxurious feel. Room 304, a "superior sea view room," is representative of Carducci 76's innovative style. The room features a large platform bed nestled between two teak-paneled walls and that stares right at a large picture window boasting a clear sea view. The room's closet and bathroom doors are made from the same wood paneling while both sides of the room feature sliding glass doors that open out onto private decks large enough for two chairs each. The three walls of windows give the room an open-air feel and with the abundance of wood, the experience is reminiscent of sleeping in a tree house. For a more traditional feel and layout, the two deluxe rooms between the turret suites are the next best options. Square-shaped rooms, they feature big white couches, dark wooden floors, clean white walls, and soft gray bed covers. The bedcover fabric used in all the rooms is actually an original fabric and design by Alberta Feretti. Both deluxe rooms have balconies that overlook the sea; French doors allow a pleasant ocean breeze to enter the room. The overall aesthetic of the rooms is simple, contemporary, and chic with a monochromatic color scheme and minimal decoration.

OPPOSITE *The turret platform bed in the Thai Suite*

OVERLEAF CLOCKWISE FROM TOP LEFT *Cattolica's famous umbrella parade; mod furnishings in the guestrooms; the 1920s villa facade; the art-deco-inspired bar; teak paneling keeps the bed neat and cozy; the exotic design of the garden*

BORGO DI BASTIA CRETI

UMBERTIDE, UMBRIA

THE thickly forested hills of the Umbrian countryside are like real-life representations of the storybook illustrations of Heidi's Switzerland—they're that big, that green, and that beautiful. Bastia Creti is a small hamlet of stone buildings located at the very top of one of the iconic peaks not far from Umbria's unofficial capital, Umbertide. The mountaintop village dates back as early as the year 1200, when it was presumed to be a monastery of nuns of Santa Lucia. Today Bastia Creti is a private *borgo* co-owned by Rome's legendary Hotel Hassler owner, Roberto E. Wirth. He inherited part of the *borgo* from his late mother, Carmen Bucher-Wirth, who was responsible for the estate's careful restoration. The refurbishment of the five buildings and chapel was done using period materials, carefully matching new stone to the beautiful surviving pink and white Assisi stone and finding replacement terra-cotta roof tiles from a similar time period.

Unmarked from the main road, the *borgo* is found only by following the precise directions provided upon booking. After turning left off the main road and onto the nondescript farm road, the trek upward begins, with the ascent continuing to the top of the mountain, where you reach the stately iron gates of the *borgo*. It is a considerable uphill journey, but the final destination does not disappoint. The sprawling lawn and gravel driveway are finely manicured and present an appropriate introduction to the *borgo*'s orderly aesthetic. The stone buildings are pleasantly ivy covered and set around an antique terra-cotta-paved courtyard that doubles as the *borgo*'s main thoroughfare down to the sprawling yard and pool beyond. The historic chapel has been remodeled into a large dining room with a long, elegant table and newly frescoed walls. The grassy terrace just outside the chapel has the best view of the rolling hills and is set up with tables for al fresco dining.

The accommodations at Borgo di Bastia Creti are scarcely advertised, found only through a villa rental company and word of mouth. The minimal publicity, along with the secluded location, preserves the property's hideaway status and ensures complete privacy for its guests. The property is usually rented in its entirety, proving a successful venue for large family reunions and private events. Though more recently, as Umbria grows in popularity, couples and families of four or five have been renting one of the three larger residences for a week's time.

The *borgo* is on six acres of beautifully landscaped property that also features a large swimming pool, a tennis court with a separate tennis backboard, and a log-cabin sauna. There is also a modernized barbecue area with seating ideal for group barbecues down by the pool. The layout of the property begs for large group gatherings and activity-filled entertainment.

The rolling hills are the backyard of the cottage at Borgo di Bastia Creti

Despite the steep driveway, leaving the property is relatively simple, and all guests are given their own electronic gate openers so they may come and go as they please. The area has some wonderful local restaurants, and cultural and historical cities like Assisi, Orvieto, and Arezzo all make pleasurable day trips. The *borgo*'s caretakers, Rita and Benito De Mattia, are a charming elderly couple who live on the property and tend to the guests and the upkeep of the estate. Rita is an excellent cook and will prepare as many meals as requested with prior reservation. She has lived on the premises since it has been in the Wirth family and is as much a fixture of the place as the ivy on the buildings.

THE ROOMS

Rooms at Borgo di Bastia Creti are divided into five separate rentals: La Limonaia, Gli Olivi, The Cottage, I Cipressi, and Le Ginestre. The largest, Le Ginestre, has four bedrooms, sleeping eight people, and has a picture-perfect dining terrace with sweeping views of the patchwork valley below. Each room has its own bathroom and double beds, which can all be converted to two single beds with a simple switch of fitted sheets. The interiors are modestly done, with the only semblance of color found in the patterned brocade canopy and bedspreads. The furniture is spartan, reminiscent of the *borgo*'s monastical roots. The second-largest house, I Cipressi, has a beautiful, ski-lodge-like open-air living room and kitchen area, divided by a massive stone fireplace accessible from both sides. I Cipressi has three bedrooms, with a center stone staircase and a particularly charming double bedroom with its own terrace. The interiors of I Cipressi are con-

siderably more colorful than those of Le Ginestre, with fabric-covered armchairs and throw pillows done in rich autumn colors. La Limonaia is the "honeymoon suite," providing the most privacy in its secluded location below the other properties and with direct access to the property's garden. Ideal for a couple alone or with a small child, La Limonaia has one bedroom with its own bathroom, and a pullout couch in the living room with separate guest bathroom. The panoramic views from La Limonaia and its own private terrace are the perfect ingredients for a romantic vacation in the hills. The Cottage is the second most private option and sleeps four people with two bedrooms. This duplex accommodation has a large master bedroom on the ground floor and second-floor double room with a private entrance. The interiors of The Cottage are similarly country quaint, though both bedrooms are spacious, with spectacular mountaintop views. The final housing option is Gli Olivi, just across from I Cipressi and above Le Ginestre. Gli Olivi has two second-floor bedrooms, one with a double and the other featuring two twin beds. Both rooms have their own bathrooms, though only the twin bedroom has a shower. The terra-cotta tile floors and simple wood furniture in the bedrooms give the rooms an authentic mountaintop feel. The first-floor living room and ample-sized kitchen are perfect for cooking, sharing meals, and ultimately settling on the comfy sofa to watch a DVD on the large flat-screen television. Perhaps it is the mountain location, the tall pine trees, or the constant cool breeze that evokes the nesting instinct, but the desire to sleep, eat, and lounge is pleasantly encouraged and easily satisfied at Borgo di Bastia Creti.

*The expansive gardens
of the Borgo*

ABOVE *Al fresco dining at Le Ginestre and fireside meals in the kitchen at I Cipressi*

OPPOSITE *Blue panels give a warm tone to the bedrooms in Le Ginestre*

APPENDIX: PROPERTY LISTINGS

Please note that all hotel information listed is subject to change, including prices that were quoted at the time of printing. Please also be aware that many hotels, especially those in the temperate zone or along the coast, close during low season (typically November through April). Check the hotel's website for the most accurate, up-to-date information.

Rate key:
200–450 Euros: moderate
450–800 Euros: luxury
800–1500 Euros: premiere

PUGLIA
Masseria Torre Coccaro
Contrada Coccaro, 8
72015 Savelletri di Fasano (Brindisi)
Tel.: (+39) 080 482 9310
Fax: (+39) 080 482 7992
www.gesthotels.com/coccaro_new/english.html
Rates: Luxury
POOL, SPA, BEACH CLUB, RESTAURANT,
COOKING CLASSES

Masseria Torre Maizza
Contrada Coccaro,
72015 Savelletri di Fasano (Brindisi)
Tel.: (+39) 080 482 7838
Fax: (+39) 080 441 4059
www.gesthotels.com/maizza/english.html
Rates: Premiere
POOL, SPA, BEACH CLUB, RESTAURANT, GOLF

La Sommita
Via Scipione Petrarolo, 7
72017 Ostuni (Puglia)
Tel.: (+39) 083 130 5925
Fax: (+39) 083 130 6729
www.lasommita.it
Rates: Moderate
RESTAURANT, BAR, SPA, BEACH, HORSEBACK RIDING

LAZIO (ROMA)
Il Palazzetto
Vicolo del Bottino, 8
00187 Roma (Roma)
Tel.: (+39) 066 993 41000
Fax: (+39) 066 991 065
www.ilpalazzettoroma.com
Rates: Moderate
BAR, RESTAURANT, WINE CLASSES

Portrait Suites
Via Bocca di Leone, 23
00187 Roma (Roma)
Tel.: (+39) 066 938 0742
Fax: (+39) 066 919 0625
www.lungarnohotels.com
Rates: Luxury
BAR, TERRACE

La Posta Vecchia
Palo Laiziale,
00055 Ladispoli (Roma)
Tel.: (+39) 069 949 501
Fax: (+39) 069 949 507
www.lapostavecchia.com
Rates: Premiere
POOL, RESTAURANT, BEAUTY CENTER, SEASIDE,
COOKING CLASSES, ART MUSEUM

CAMPANIA (LA COSTIERA AMALFITANA, CAPRI, & ISCHIA)
Casa Angelina
Via G. Capirglione, 147
84010 Praiano (Salerno)
Tel.: (+39) 089 813 1333
Fax: (+39) 089 874 266
www.casangelina.com
Rates: Moderate to Luxury
POOL, SEASIDE, BEACH, RESTAURANT, INDOOR
POOL/GYM

Villa Cimbrone
Via S. Chiara, 26
84010 Ravello (Salerno)
Tel.: (+39) 089 857 459
Fax: (+39) 089 857 777
www.villacimbrone.com
Rates: Luxury
POOL, VIEW, RESTAURANT, BOTANICAL GARDENS

JK Capri
Via Provinciale Marina Grande, 225
80073 Capri (Napoli)
Tel.: (+39) 081 838 4001
Fax: (+39) 081 837 0438
www.jkcapri.com
Rates: Luxury to Premiere
POOL, SPA, BEACH, VIEW, RESTAURANT, BAR

Mezzatorre
Via Mezzatorre, 23
80075 Forio d'Ischia (Napoli)
Tel.: (+39) 081 986 111
Fax: (+39) 081 986 015
www.mezzatorre.it
Rates: Luxury
POOL, SEASIDE, VIEW, RESTAURANT, GYM, SPA

TOSCANA
Castello del Nero
L'Orto del Forte S.p.A. Strada Spicciano, 7
50028 Tavarnelle Val di Pesa (Firenze)
Tel.: (+39) 055 806 470
Fax: (+39) 055 806 47777
www.castello-del-nero.com
Rates: Luxury to Premiere
POOL, RESTAURANT, GYM, SPA

Villa Mangiacane
Via Faltignano, 4
50026 San Casciano, (Firenze)
Tel.: (+39) 055 829 0123
Fax: (+39) 055 829 0358
www.mangiacane.com
Rates: Luxury to Premiere
POOLS, SPA, RESTAURANT, LOUNGE BAR, GYM,
VINEYARDS

*Villa Fontelunga and Villa Scanagallo, Villa Gallo,
and Villa Galletto*
Via Cunicchio, 5
Localita Pozzo
52045 Foiano della Chiana, (Arezzo)
Tel.: (+39) 057 566 0410
Fax: (+39) 0575 661 963
www.fontelunga.com
Rates: Villa Fontelunga: Moderate
   Galletto villa: Luxury
   Gallo villa: Luxury
   Scannagallo villa: Premiere
   Fontelunga villa: Luxury
POOL, TWICE-WEEKLY DINNER

Villa Castelletto
Loc. Castelletto
Monticchiello, (SI) 53020
Rental agency: Your Tuscany
Tel.: (+39) 066 880 9301
Fax: (+39) 066 892 771
www.yourtuscany.com
Luxury
POOL, GARDENS

Castello Banfi: Il Borgo
Castello di Poggio Alle Mura, 1
Montalcino (SI) 53024
Tel.: (+39) 057 787 7700
Fax: (+39) 057 787 7701
www.castellobanfi.com
Rates: Luxury
POOL, RESTAURANT, VINEYARDS, WINE CLASSES,
COOKING CLASSES

Castello di Vicarello
Loc. Vicarello, 1 Poggi del Sasso
58044 Grosetto (Toscana)
Tel.: (+39) 056 499 0718 (no fax)
www.castellodivicarello.it
Rates: Luxury
POOLS, MEALS INCLUDED, VINEYARDS, GARDENS,
HUNTING, COOKING CLASSES

Il Falconière
Localita S. Martino, 370
52044 Cortona (Arezzo)
Tel.: (+39) 057 561 2679
Fax: (+39) 057 561 2927
www.ilfalconiere.com
Rates: Luxury
POOLS, RESTAURANT, VINEYARDS, COOKING CLASSES

Albergo Villa Marta
Via del Ponte Guasperini, 873
55100 Lucca Toscana
Tel.: (+39) 058 337 0101
Fax: (+39) 058 337 9999
www.albergovillamarta.it
Rates: Moderate
POOL, RESTAURANT, COOKING CLASSES

La Bandita
Podere La Bandita,
53026 Pienza (SI),
Tel.: (+39) 333 404 6704
Fax: +1-212-202-622
www.la-bandita.com
Rates: Moderate
POOL, TWICE-WEEKLY DINNER

Villa Cabbiavoli
Via Del Vallone
Castel Fiorentino, *Firenze*
Rental agency: Your Tuscany
Tel.: (+39) 066 880 9301
Fax: (+39) 066 892 771
www.yourtuscany.com
Rates: Luxury
POOL, VINEYARDS

FIRENZE
Hotel Lungarno
Borgo San Jacopo, 14
50214 Firenze
Tel.: (+39) 055 27264000
Fax: (+39) 055 268 431
www.lungarnohotels.com
Rates: Luxury
RESTAURANT, BAR, RIVER VIEW

Torre di Bellosguardo
Via Roti Michelozzi, 2
50124 Firenze
Tel.: (+39) 055 229 8145
Fax: (+39) 055 229 008
Rates: Moderate
POOL, GARDENS

UMBRIA
Borgo di Bastia Creti
Fa. Spedalicchio
06019 Umbertide (Perugia)
CV Travel
Tel.: 1-866-587-9395
italy@cvtravel.co.uk
Rates: Le Ginestre (8 people): Luxury
   I Cipressi (6 people): Luxury
   Cottage (6 people): Luxury
   Gli Olivi (4 people): Moderate
   La Limonaia (2 people): Moderate
   La Capella (8 people): Luxury
   Entire Borgo (26 people): Luxury
POOL, TENNIS COURT, MEALS UPON REQUEST, SAUNA

LE MARCHE
Carducci 76
Viale Carducci, 76
47841 Cattolica (Rn)
Tel.: (+39) 054 195 4677
Fax: (+39) 054 183 1557
www.carducci76.it
Rates: Moderate
POOL, SEASIDE, BEACH CLUB, RESTAURANT, SPA

VENEZIA
Ca Maria Adele
Dorsoduro, 111
30123 Venezia
Tel.: (+39) 041 520 3078
Fax: (+39) 041 528 9013
www.camariaadele.it
Rates: Moderate
CONCIERGE, BREAKFAST

Palazzo Bauer
San Marco, 1459
30124 Venezia
Tel.: (+39) 041 520 7022
Fax: (+39) 041 520 7557
www.bauerhotels.com
Rates: Luxury to Premiere
RESTAURANT, GYM, SPA

Palazzo Mocenigo
Calle corner, San Marco, 3362
30124 Venezia
Tel.: (+39) 041 520 7022
Fax: (+39) 041 520 7557
www.bauerhotels.com
Rates: Premiere
VIEW, WATER ACCESS, PRIVATE STAFF UPON REQUEST

PIEMONTE
La Villa Hotel
Via Torino, 7
14046 Mombaruzzo (Piemonte)
Tel.: (+39) 014 179 3890
Fax: (+39) 014 173 9991
www.lavillahotel.net
Rates: Moderate
POOL, VINEYARDS, RESTAURANT, VIEW

Villa Beccaris
Via Bava Beccaris, 1
12065 Monforte d'Alba (CN)
Tel.: (+39) 017 378 158
Fax: (+39) 017 378 190
www.villabeccaris.it
Rates: Moderate
POOL, VINEYARDS, VIEW, ENOTECA

Villa Tiboldi
Case Sparse, 127
12043 Canale (CN)
Tel.: (+39) 017 397 0388
Fax: (+39) 017 395 9233
www.villatiboldi.it
Rates: Moderate
POOL, VINEYARDS, RESTAURANT, WINE CANTINA

LAKES
Grand Hotel Villa Serbelloni
Via Roma, 1
22021 Bellagio (Como)
Tel.: (+39) 031 950 216
Fax: (+39) 031 951 529
www.villaserbelloni.com
Rates: Luxury to Premiere
POOL, TENNIS COURTS, GYM, SQUASH COURTS,
BEACH, RESTAURANT, LAKESIDE, SPA

ACKNOWLEDGMENTS

I want to thank all my friends and my family who supported me through this exciting but demanding adventure. Thank you to all the hotels I had the pleasure of visiting, and to AutoEurope for getting me there. And to my editor Kathleen Jayes, my publisher Charles Miers, my high-spirited photographer David Cicconi and assistant José Bernad. I'd also like to credit Peter Webster, Tom Edelman, and Roberto Coin with helping ensure this project's success. And last to Friso van Reesema, whose love and support kept me balanced from start to finish.

ABOUT THE AUTHOR

MEG NOLAN is a writer and editor in New York City. She began her career as the Washington producer for NBC's Chris Matthews but left to pursue print journalism. Since then she has worked at *Vanity Fair* and *Travel + Leisure Golf* and her work has appeared in *Italy Weekly*, *Golf for Women*, and *Philadelphia/DC Style*. But it was her position with the *International Herald Tribune* in Milan that brought her one step closer to her ultimate goal of spending as much time as possible in Italy.

DAVID CICCONI is the former Photo Editor at *Travel + Leisure*. During his time there, the magazine received over 20 awards for excellence in photography. As a photographer, he has shot for *Travel + Leisure*, *Conde Nast Traveller UK*, *Food & Wine*, and *W Magazine*. In 2006, he was chosen as one of Photo District News' 30 Emerging Photographers.

MELISSA BIGGS BRADLEY is the founder and CEO of Indagare, a new luxury travel site. For almost twelve years, Melissa was the travel editor at *Town & Country*, where she also served as the features editor. In 2003, she launched *Town & Country Travel*, which, under her editorship in 2006, was nominated for a National Magazine Award for General Excellence by the American Society of Magazine Editors (ASME).